SKILLS

SKILLS

Ian J Cross MA (Cantab), Solicitor

Andrew T Gibson MA (Cantab), Solicitor, ATII

Rachel Hawes MA (Oxon), Solicitor

Martin Iller LLB (Nottingham), Solicitor

Carol S Moore LLB (London), Solicitor

Peter Mott, Solicitor

Michael Petley BA (Cantab), Solicitor

Allun D Thomas LLB (London), Solicitor

Victor C Tonge LLB (Nottingham), Solicitor

JORDANS

1993

Published by
Jordan Publishing Limited
21 St Thomas Street
Bristol BS1 6JS

British Library Cataloguing-in-Publication Data
A catalogue record for this book is available from the British Library.

ISBN 0 85308 195 6

Photoset by Pentacor PLC, High Wycombe, Buckinghamshire
Printed in Great Britain by BPCC Books and Journals Ltd, Exeter

PREFACE

Knowledge of how the internal combustion engine works and what the Highway Code states does not necessarily make a good driver. In the same way, the practice of law requires not merely an understanding of law and procedure but also the ability to perform a number of legal skills.

This Resource Book covers five legal skills:

(1) writing and drafting;
(2) legal research;
(3) interviewing and advising;
(4) negotiation; and
(5) advocacy.

The chapters covering each of these skills are essential preparatory reading for practice of the relevant skill on the Legal Practice Course.

The book will also help you in your early years as a trainee or qualified solicitor, both to monitor your own development and to evaluate others, learning from their successes and their failures.

The chapters in Part III on interviewing and advising, negotiation and advocacy, all of which involve the use of oral communication skills, are largely based on Continuing Education courses which The College of Law has run for the solicitors' profession for a number of years. In mounting the interviewing and negotiating courses, the College received invaluable assistance from Dr Karl Mackie (now Chief Executive of the Centre for Dispute Resolution). Similarly, the courses on advocacy benefited greatly from the advice and help of His Honour Judge Groves, Her Honour Judge Marian Norrie, His Honour Judge Nigel Fricker QC and Tony Edwards, solicitor. In addition, the many solicitors who have attended the courses have contributed their know how to them, and therefore also to these chapters.

The College of Law is also grateful to members of its Advocacy Advisory Board for their helpful comments and suggestions on the advocacy chapter.

MICHAEL PETLEY
Chester

CONTENTS

PART I

WRITING AND DRAFTING

Chapter 1

WRITING AND DRAFTING

1.1 INTRODUCTION

Chapter 1 contents

1.1.1 A solicitor's written skills

This chapter aims to provide an introduction to the skills required by a solicitor when writing letters, reports and memoranda, and drafting legal documents.

1.1.2 How to approach this material

The notes which follow are intended to encourage you to think about the way in which you write and draft. You should apply these principles, where relevant, throughout all the subjects on the Legal Practice Course, not merely in exercises designed specifically to test writing and drafting. The principles of legal drafting will be further expanded in relation to the types of legal document relevant to individual subjects. You may find, however, that some solicitors' firms have their own style guides and precedents which they require you to follow, regardless of other recommendations.

1.2 SOME POINTS ON STYLE

One critic has said of the legal profession: 'Lawyers have two common failings. One is that they do not write well and the other is that they think they do'.

This chapter encourages you to write in plain English and to avoid using unnecessarily complex expressions.

1.2.1 Verbiage – some danger areas

'Padding'

Try to avoid the use of unnecessary phrases which lengthen the sentence while adding nothing to its meaning. For example:

- 'until such time as'
- 'in this instance'
- 'the fact that'
- 'of course'.

Too many adjectives?

Consider whether the noun requires an adjective at all. In the following examples the adjective adds nothing to the noun:

- 'true facts'
- 'terrible disaster'
- 'unfilled vacancy'.

Try to avoid a string of similar adjectives which do not make the meaning more precise. For example:

- 'grave and fatal error'
- 'careful and detailed consideration'

Compound prepositions
Try to avoid using a phrase where a single preposition will do. For example:

- 'in accordance with' (by, under)
- 'by reason of' (by, through)
- 'with reference to' (about)
- 'in order to' (to)

Nouns derived from verbs
Could you use the verb itself rather than a noun derived from it? (This often creates a more immediate effect.)

- 'make an admission' (admit)
- 'give consideration to' (consider)
- 'effect a termination' (terminate or end)

1.2.2 Verbs in the passive

Active and passive voice
In a sentence where the verb is in the active voice, the subject of the sentence acts upon the object of the sentence. Where the verb is in the passive voice the object of the sentence is acted upon by the subject. Compare:

> 'The defendant struck the plaintiff' (active voice).
>
> 'The plaintiff was struck by the defendant' (passive voice).

Problems with the passive
Over-use of the passive voice lengthens a sentence and can make it sound weak. In the worst cases it obscures meaning. For example:

> 'It is hoped that resources will be relocated so that changes may be made in the methods by which the system is administered.'

Where the verb is in the passive you may accidentally omit the phrase which indicates who or what is doing the acting. For example:

> 'The plaintiff was struck.'

In a legal context, the effect of this omission may be important. For example:

> 'Notice will be served.' By whom?

Some uses for the passive
The passive can sound more objective and detached and therefore more appropriate in certain legal contexts. For example:

'The allegations are denied'

sounds better than

'Our client denies the allegations', which introduces a personal note.

It is correct to use the passive where the subject of the legal action is irrelevant. For example:

'The common seal of X Co was affixed . . .' It does not matter who affixed it.

The passive can also be used in a legal context to cover the possibility of action by a number of different persons, some of whom are unknown. For example:

'If the goods are damaged we will refund the cost.' This could cover damage by, the supplier, the carrier, or any third party.

1.2.3 Which word to choose?

Unfamiliar words

Is the word you have chosen unnecessarily complex? Unfamiliar words can distract the reader and create a pompous style. For example:

- 'expedite'
- 'activate'
- 'utilise'
- 'eventuality'
- 'elucidate'

Jargon

Try to avoid jargon unless you are sure the recipient will be familiar with it. For example:

- 'mortgage-sourcing information'
- 'clothing-optional beaches'

'Legalese'

If possible, avoid archaic words and phrases such as:

- 'herewith'
- 'herein'
- 'hereinbefore'
- 'hereby'
- 'crave leave'
- 'the said . . .'

Legal terms

Legal terms should be translated for lay clients. For example:

- 'joint tenancy'
- 'decree nisi'

Unnecessary word pairs
Historically, English lawyers have used Latin, Norman French and Old and Middle English for legal documents. The word pairs found in legal writing are often a French or Latin word plus its English equivalent. Where this is so, one word alone is sufficient. Examples include:

- 'null and void' (Latin/English)
- 'act and deed' (French/English)
- 'settle and compromise' (English/French)
- 'Will and Testament' (English/Latin)

1.2.4 Sentence structure

Use short sentences
In long sentences the verb, subject and object may be separated by too many sub-clauses. This places a strain on the reader's memory and understanding. Consider, for example:

> 'The evidence, including evidence from independent surveys as well as that gathered personally by the writers of this report and the results of investigations formally commissioned by this department, suggests that the public, while acknowledging an overall increase in the actual level of government spending on health, by which is meant on health care both at the doctor-patient level and in hospitals, still views the problems and defects in the National Health Service and in particular in National Health hospitals as the result of a general lack of funding.'

The sub-clauses break up the main thought of the paragraph so that it is difficult to follow. The paragraph would be better rewritten in separate sentences with the main thought first, even though this may increase its length. Brackets can be used for subsidiary points where appropriate. For example:

> 'The evidence suggests that the public still views the problems and defects in the National Health Service and in particular in National Health hospitals as the result of a general lack of funding. This is so even though it acknowledges an overall increase in the actual level of government spending on health care both at the doctor-patient level and in hospitals. (Evidence on this issue includes evidence from independent surveys, that gathered personally by the writers of this report and the results of investigations formally commissioned by this department.)'

Take care with word order
Words or phrases in the wrong place may create ambiguity.

Consider the sentence:

> 'We undertake to repair or replace goods shown to be defective *within six months.*'

It is not clear whether the phrase in italics governs the repair/replacement or the notification of defect. It could be rewritten as:

> 'Where, within six months (of the date of purchase?), goods are shown to be

defective, we will repair or replace them' (assuming this was the intended meaning).

1.2.5 Layout and presentation

Paragraphs

Using paragraphs makes prose more readable and helps to avoid cumbersome clauses and sub-clauses.

Tabulation

Tabulation may help to avoid ambiguity.

Consider the sentence:

> 'Any trainee solicitor is entitled to paid leave to attend a conference, lecture, or seminar *provided by The Law Society.*'

How much of the sentence is the phrase in italics intended to qualify? Does it apply only to 'seminar', or to 'conference' and 'lecture' as well?

Compare:

> 'Any trainee solicitor is entitled to paid leave to attend:
>
> (a) a conference; or
> (b) a lecture; or
> (c) a seminar,
>
> provided by The Law Society.'

Care should be taken, however, not to indent the final phrase 'provided by The Law Society' to the same margin as 'a seminar' or the ambiguity would remain.

Numbering

Where a series of points is being made, numbering may improve clarity and aid later cross-referencing.

Examples of numbering systems:

4.5.1 The system adopted in this Resource Book and known as the decimal system.

4(5)(a)(i) A system based on the legislative approach and known as the alpha-numeric system.

4.5(a)(i) A combination system using elements of both decimal and alpha-numeric systems.

1.3 WRITING LETTERS

1.3.1 Who is the addressee?

Consider the needs of the reader and try to adapt your style accordingly.

The lay client

Take care to avoid jargon and legalese when writing to a lay client. Explain all unfamiliar terms, but try not to make the tone patronising. How familiar is the client with the subject?

The business client
The business client will generally be familiar with solicitors' letters, so avoid verbosity and get to the point quickly.

Other professionals
Other professionals may need some legal terms translated.

Other solicitors
What kind of matter are you dealing with? Are you writing from a position of strength or weakness? Do you want to adopt a conciliatory or non-conciliatory stance? Consider which is more likely to persuade the addressee. Remember that the other solicitor may send a copy of your letter to his client.

1.3.2 'Ghosting'

You may be asked to write letters to be signed in a partner's own name. Read the file and consider the partner's style. Check how well the partner knows the addressee; for example, if you are writing to a client, is the partner on first-name terms with him?

1.3.3 Starting and ending the letter

Generally
Letters beginning 'Dear Sirs/Sir/Madam' all end 'Yours faithfully'.

A letter addressed to a person by surname, eg 'Dear Mr Smith', ends with 'Yours sincerely'.

A letter beginning 'Dear John' may end with 'Yours sincerely' or 'Yours' (either of which could be prefixed by a phrase such as 'Kind regards' or 'Best wishes').

Female addressees
Where possible, try to find out a woman's preference in advance, for example 'Miss', 'Mrs', or 'Ms'. As an alternative, some writers use 'Dear Jane Smith' if 'Dear Madam' would be too formal and 'Dear Jane' too informal.

1.3.4 Content

Consider overall structure
An initial heading identifying the matter is conventional. For example:

Jones to Smith
Sale of 25 Acacia Avenue, Bristol

A complex letter will be easier to understand (and reply to) if you give each paragraph a number and a heading.

Form and style
If you are writing in the firm's name (eg a formal letter to the other side), write in the first person plural ('we') and be consistent.

Acknowledge the addressee's last communication.

If it is your first letter to the addressee, explain your involvement.

State the purpose of the letter.

Carry out that purpose using:

- logical sequence
- separate paragraphs
- short sentences
- active voice

Write in a restrained tone. Avoid over-emphasis (eg unnecessary adverbs – 'totally unhappy', 'completely inaccurate'). Use exclamation marks sparingly. Do not express surprise, amazement, outrage, etc.

Avoid jokes and witticisms.

1.3.5 Some practical points

Second thoughts and improvements
Try to be detached about your letter. How will it appear through another's eyes?

How would it sound if read out in open court in the future?

Try not to write a letter in a temper or in an emotional state. If you do, do not post it until you have had a chance to re-read it or a colleague has reviewed it.

Consider giving a deadline for a reply (eg if the matter is urgent or if the letter might be unwelcome).

If you have asked a client to do something, are your instructions clear?

Check the grammar and spelling.

Final checks
Check that the letter:

- carries the correct references (ie yours and those of the other side)
- is dated
- is signed
- is accompanied by the right enclosures
- is put into the right envelope, and is properly addressed

1.4 WRITING REPORTS AND MEMORANDA

1.4.1 Reports

Purpose
Reports usually cover a specific subject and serve a particular purpose. In the office you may have to write a report on some legal research or fact-finding you were asked to undertake.

Is your research complete?
Consider whether you have all the necessary information and identify any gaps.

Edit your material

Consider how much information should go into the report. Brevity increases the likelihood of the report being read, but too little information may not adequately support your conclusions.

Contents

Consider including:

- a contents page or index
- an introduction explaining why the report was commissioned
- a brief summary of the report before the main text for quick reference
- diagrams (if relevant)
- case or statute references (if relevant)
- a bibliography
- appendices
- acknowledgments of sources of information

Structure

Plan the text of your report carefully to produce a logical argument.

Have you done what you were asked to do? Have you reached a conclusion? Have you identified options?

Style

For whom are you writing? Adapt your style appropriately.

Consider whether you should paraphrase or explain your source material, or whether you can reproduce it word for word.

Have the report typed in draft form first and read it through carefully, amending and re-writing where necessary.

Layout and presentation

Make sure the report is well set out, with clear headings and numbered paragraphs and sub-paragraphs if appropriate.

Is it to be used as a discussion document? If so, consider having it typed in double spacing with wide margins to leave room for others to write notes.

1.4.2 Memoranda

Types of memoranda

Solicitors generally have to write two types of memoranda:

- attendance notes (as a record of their meetings or telephone calls with clients, other solicitors, etc)
- internal memoranda (as a quick way of communicating with others in the firm)

Attendance notes

Attendance notes are put on a file as a record of an oral discussion, transaction or agreement and must be clear and accurate in case of any later dispute.

They are essential for anyone who takes over a file and was not present for the meeting, telephone call etc.

They may also be needed when a client's bill is prepared as part of the record of chargeable time spent on the matter.

Write or dictate your attendance note as soon as possible after the event it records so as to avoid forgetting essential detail.

Always try to take contemporaneous notes – in a simple case you can put them straight on the file. For more complicated matters, you can use your notes to compile your attendance note, but do not destroy them; they are important additional evidence in any dispute.

An attendance note should normally contain the following:

- the client's name
- the subject matter
- your reference
- the date
- the place (of any meeting)
- the people present (at a meeting)
- the starting and finishing times (of the meeting or phone call)
- a summary of what was discussed or agreed
- any follow-up action to be taken by you or others

If your attendance note records an important decision or agreement, always confirm it by letter to avoid misunderstandings.

Internal memoranda

Keep internal memoranda brief and business-like, but take care with the tone. If a memo sounds curt, you may cause offence to the recipient.

The format required is generally as follows:

MEMORANDUM

From:

To:

Fee earner's reference:

Date:

Client's name:

Client's matter:

File number:

Most firms use printed forms on which these headings already appear.

1.5 LEGAL DRAFTING: BASIC PRINCIPLES

1.5.1 What are your aims when drafting?

The aims of drafting are to produce a document which is unambiguous, easy to read and understand, and an accurate reflection of the client's instructions.

Unambiguous

There is always a risk that a court will have to construe the document.

Take care that you use words and terms which have been legally defined only in their defined meaning.

Easy to read and understand

Take care with form and layout of a document. This will not only make it more aesthetically pleasing and easy to use, but can make its meaning clearer.

An accurate reflection of the client's instructions

Are you sure you understand what the transaction involves? For example, if the document is to deal with a commercial process, do you understand that process?

Are you clear what kind of document the client wants? For example, is it a standard-form agreement intended to be reused, or is it for one particular transaction?

1.5.2 The structure of a document

The structure of a legal document will vary depending on its nature, but many documents will contain the following elements:

- commencement
- date
- parties
- recitals
- operative part
- testimonium
- schedules
- execution and attestation

Commencement, date and parties

A document will normally begin with a 'commencement' which describes the nature of the document, for example 'This Agreement', 'This Conveyance'. Alternatively, the document's title can simply be printed as a heading. Deeds may also use the word 'deed' in the title, eg 'This deed of Conveyance'.

A space should be left for insertion of the date when the document is completed.

The full names and addresses of the parties should be inserted. (In the case of a company the address of its registered office should be inserted.)

Example

SERVICE AGREEMENT

DATE:

PARTIES: (1) Weyford Products Limited whose registered office is at 32 Bridge House, Wharf Road, Milton, Berefordshire.

(2) Joan Alice Bennet of 8 High Street, Milton, Berefordshire.

A long and complicated document can benefit from an index or table of clauses (preferably at the front).

Recitals

Recitals clauses are not essential and you should consider carefully whether or not to include them. You can use them to set out the background facts to the document and so make it more self-explanatory. For example, in a conveyance of land by a personal representative the date of the deceased's death and the date on which a grant of representation was obtained could be recited.

Recitals are also sometimes used to introduce and summarise the contents of the operative part of the document but, except in complicated documents, this is generally not necessary and increases the risk of introducing ambiguities.

Operative part

The operative part of a document is the part which creates the legal rights and obligations. It may contain the following types of clauses.

DEFINITIONS

Definitions can serve three functions in a document. They may be used:

(1) as a form of shorthand to avoid needless repetition. For example:

'72 Shrewbridge Road
Malbank, Daleshire
('the Property')';

(2) as a detailed explanation of a term used in the document. For example:

'In this Agreement the Period of Hire means from (but not including) 28th November 19– until (and including) 20th December 19–';

(3) to widen or narrow a word's normal meaning. For example:

'In this clause "Boat" includes sail-board', (where the term 'Boat' has been defined differently elsewhere in the document).

If it is necessary to define a term, consider whether the definition is to apply throughout the whole document or only within a particular clause; in the latter case, it could be defined in that clause.

The clause giving definitions which are intended to apply throughout the whole document should come first in the operative part of the document, with the definitions set out in alphabetical order.

Do not define a term by reference to another, undefined, term. For example:

'In this Agreement Property includes preliminary and reserved options' ('preliminary' and 'reserved' options being undefined terms).

Use a capital letter throughout the document for the first letter of a defined word or phrase, but only where the word or phrase is being used in its defined meaning.

OTHER OPERATIVE PROVISIONS

The other operative clauses of the document will be determined by the nature of the document. For example, a commercial agreement will generally contain:

- conditions precedent (setting out conditions which have to be satisfied before the agreement comes into force)
- agreements (setting out the rights and obligations of the parties)
- representations and warranties (ie statements about factual and legal matters which one of the parties requires to be made to him in a legally binding way)
- 'boiler-plate' clauses (ie standard clauses inserted into all agreements of such type dealing with, for example, the service of notices under the agreement, or the jurisdiction for action where the agreement has an international element)

STRUCTURING THE OPERATIVE PART

How the operative part is structured will depend on the nature of the document.

A chronological order may be appropriate to some documents. For example, in an employment contract the appropriate order might be:

- appointment to job
- period of appointment
- duties
- remuneration
- holidays
- sickness
- dismissal, etc

Other documents may fall conveniently into two (or perhaps four) major sections. For example, in a hiring agreement:

- Owner's Rights and Obligations
- Hirer's Rights and Obligations

STRUCTURING CLAUSES AND SUB-CLAUSES WITHIN THE OPERATIVE PART

Set out the detail of the document neatly with plenty of space and appropriate indentation.

Use a separate clause for each separate matter.

Use sub-paragraphing to avoid long, cumbersome clauses and provisos.

Consider:

'1. The Licensee shall purchase exclusively from the Grantor all materials used in making the Invention PROVIDED that the Licensee shall be entitled to relieve itself of its liability to observe this obligation upon giving the Grantor three months' notice in writing.'

Compare:

'1. Subject to Clause 2, the Licensee shall purchase exclusively from the Grantor all materials used in making the Invention.

2. The Licensee may end the obligation contained in Clause 1 by giving the Grantor three months' notice in writing.'

Number each clause and sub-clause.

Give each clause or group of clauses a heading. For example:

'TENANT'S COVENANTS'

Consider using a clause such as:

'The heading and marginal notes are for convenience only and do not affect the interpretation of this agreement.'

Be prepared to use traditional punctuation in the usual way. Excessive use of commas can lead to ambiguity if it is not clear how they are paired, but a proper use of commas can assist understanding.

Examples

- in a list: 'black, pink, blue, brown, green and yellow'
- to separate a qualifying condition from the main sentence: 'If, before the Completion Date of this Agreement, the Property is damaged or destroyed by fire . . .'

Testimonium

A testimonium clause is not essential but, if used, it introduces the signatures of the parties and may describe a particular method of executing where, for example, a company is using its seal as part of its execution, or an attorney is signing on behalf of a party.

Schedules

Use schedules where appropriate to avoid breaking the continuity of a document with too much detail. The operative part of the document then refers to the schedule, and the schedule contains the detail. For example:

'TENANT'S COVENANTS

The Tenant covenants with the Landlord to observe and perform the covenants set out in Schedule 1.

SCHEDULE 1

1. To pay the rent . . . etc.'

Execution and attestation

A document will end with an execution clause. This will refer to the signatures of the parties and any other formalities necessary to give the document legal effect. The wording of this clause will vary depending on the nature of the party executing, whether the document is executed as a deed, and whether the party's signature is witnessed ('attested').

For a document executed by an individual and not intended to take effect as a deed the clause could read:

Signed by ALAN JONES) in the presence of:)	(Alan Jones signs here)

(Witness signs here)

If the document is intended to take effect as a deed the clause could read:

Executed as a deed) by ALAN JONES) in the presence of:)	(Alan Jones signs here)

(Witness signs here)

1.5.3 Some drafting pitfalls

Do you mean 'and' or 'or'?

Consider:

> 'The Seller may serve notice of termination, recover goods already delivered and retain all instalments already paid.'

The use of 'and' in this sentence suggests that the list is conjunctive, ie that the seller may do all of the things in it. But can he choose to do only some of them?

Compare:

> 'The Seller may serve notice of termination, recover goods already delivered or retain all instalments already paid.'

The use of 'or' here suggests that the list is disjunctive, ie that the seller may do only one of the things in the list. But it could also mean that he may *both* serve notice *and* either recover goods or retain instalments.

To avoid such ambiguity, consider (depending on the meaning required) using phrases such as:

> 'The Seller may do all or any of the following:'

or

> 'The Seller may exercise one only of the following rights:'.

The 'undistributed middle'

Take care with provisions 'before/after' a particular date or 'over/under' a particular weight or measure.

Consider the following examples:

> 'Where the company delivers the goods before 1 January . . . / Where the company delivers the goods after 1 January . . .'

What happens if it delivers them *on* 1 January?

> 'Goods over 40lb must be sent by rail . . . / Goods under 40lb may be sent by air'

What about goods weighing *exactly* 40lb?

Expressions of time

Take care to avoid ambiguity.

Consider:

> 'The Buyer must pay a deposit within 7 days of today's date.'

Does the 7 days include or exclude today?

For legal and practical reasons, avoid expressing periods of time in the following ways:

- from [a date]
- by [a date]
- within [so many days of] or from [a date]
- until [a date]

It is safer to be clear by using one of the following:

- from but excluding/not including
- from and including
- on or after
- on or before
- within a period of 7 days commencing with
- until but excluding/not including
- until and including

Are you creating an obligation or a discretion?

An obligation is created by the phrase:

> 'The Customer shall pay a deposit on signing this Agreement.'

A discretion is created by the phrase:

> 'The Company may retain the deposit if the Customer does not collect the goods on or before 30 June.'

Take care when using 'shall'. It is grammatically correct to use it in the third person to indicate an obligation ('the Tenant shall pay the Rent') but it can also be used in the first person to indicate simple future ('I shall go to London'). Alternatively, you could use 'must' to create an obligation.

Avoid words of similar sound or appearance

Words of similar sound or appearance can be accidentally transposed by a typist and may also confuse a lay client. For example:

Avoid	*Use instead*
'mortgagor/mortgagee'	'lender/borrower'
'lessor/lessee'	'landlord/tenant'

Ambiguous pronouns

Consider:

> 'Where the Supplier fails to deliver the Goods to the Customer in accordance with Clause 9 or the Goods delivered do not correspond with the sample he may terminate this Agreement.'
>
> Who may terminate the agreement?

Where it is not clear to which noun a pronoun refers, the noun should be repeated.

The eiusdem generis rule

Consider:

> 'In consequence of war, disturbance or any other cause.'

Unless a contrary intention appears, 'any other cause' will be construed as meaning only causes in the same category as those previously listed.

To avoid ambiguity, add (as appropriate):

> 'whether of the same kind as [the causes] previously listed or not' or
>
> 'or any other [cause] provided it is of the same kind as the [causes] previously listed'.

Blanks

Try to minimise the number of blanks for completion to reduce the risk that they are left uncompleted.

1.5.4 Style

Avoid 'legalese'.

If consulting more than one precedent, ensure that you produce a consistent style for your document.

If necessary, check in a legal dictionary terms which have been legally defined.

1.5.5 Clause construction

Consider:

> 'The Company shall reimburse the Replacement Value provided that the value of the claim does not exceed £1,000 and the Policyholder notifies the loss within 7 days from (but excluding) the date of its occurrence PROVIDED ALWAYS THAT the above shall not apply to claims made under Clause 10 of this Policy.'

This clause starts with a statement of a legal obligation which at first sight appears absolute. The conditions and exceptions attaching to the obligation are not stated until afterwards, so that it is necessary to reconsider the obligation in the light of them. This kind of clause construction is very common in legal drafting but it is not the most logical way to structure a clause and it makes it more difficult to understand.

In 1843, George Coode wrote a treatise on 'Legislative Expression; or, the Language of The Written Law'. His general principle is that a clause should be structured in the following order:

(1) Refer to any exceptions first: eg 'Subject to . . .'.

(2) Next, set out the circumstance or conditions upon which the legal right or obligation depends, using the present tense: eg 'If X does [. . .] and Y does [. . .]'.

(3) Next, set out the right or obligation using the active and avoiding the passive: eg 'X shall do 1, 2, 3, 4 and 5'.

(4) Finally, put the provision into paragraphs and give it a heading.

For example:

'POLICYHOLDER'S RIGHT TO REPLACEMENT VALUE

Except in the case of claims made under Clause 10 of this Policy, where:

(a) the value of the claim does not exceed £1,000; and
(b) the Policyholder notifies the loss within 7 days from (but excluding) the date of its occurrence,

the Company shall reimburse the Replacement Value.'

1.5.6 How do you approach drafting a document?

Some documents are entirely conventional in form and use of a precedent may be unavoidable; others give more scope for individual drafting 'from scratch'.

Practical hints for drafting 'from scratch'

First 'brainstorm', ie produce a list of all possible points you think the document should cover.

Arrange those points under headings.

Put the headings into a logical order.

Consult a precedent to see if you have overlooked anything.

Expand the points under the headings into clauses and sub-clauses.

If time permits, leave the draft for a while. Come back to it afresh and be critical.

Guidelines for using precedents

Try to consult several sets of precedents to see what different approaches are available.

Some precedents may be broadly based, others very specialised. Consider what your transaction requires and do not choose a more complex precedent than is necessary; for example, a simple will giving an entire estate absolutely to an adult may not need lengthy administrative provisions.

Always use the most up-to-date precedents and consult any supplements provided, especially in areas where the law changes rapidly, such as tax.

For some simple transactions, it may be possible to use a precedent without alteration, but generally you will need to adapt it.

Make sure that you understand the legal implications of the clauses you are using and know what, if any, difference the amendments you make will have. (Most precedents have explanatory notes attached. Read them carefully.)

You may have to put together clauses from different sets of precedents. Take care to amend them to achieve a uniform style.

If you have taken clauses from different precedents, make sure that all terms are defined consistently in your final draft.

Points to look out for when checking your draft

If you have altered the order of clauses or inserted additional clauses have you renumbered correctly?

If you have renumbered, have cross-references to other clauses by number become incorrect?

Have defined terms been given capital letters throughout the document?

Are the names of the parties correctly spelt?

Are figures and dates correct?

Do you have a style guide and, if so, does the document comply with it?

1.5.7 Practical and ethical considerations when drafting

Good practice when submitting a draft

Out of courtesy, you should always supply to the other side an additional copy of any draft sent for approval.

Use a layout which helps the other side to read and amend the draft; for example, use wide margins and double spacing.

Good practice when amending the other side's draft

Amend a draft by hand so that the amendments are clear. Do not have the draft retyped or the amendments will become difficult for the other side to identify.

Do not erase another firm's word processor identification markings. It will be important for them to identify the disk quickly.

If you receive a draft which is substantially acceptable but in a style of drafting which you do not favour it is tactless to redraft it in a different style and will not improve relations with that firm. The most you can do is to correct any errors and hope that any draft you send them in the future may influence them to change their style!

Ethical considerations when negotiating a draft

Two rules of professional conduct are relevant.

(1) A solicitor must not act, whether in his professional capacity or otherwise, towards anyone in a way which is fraudulent, deceitful or otherwise contrary to his position as a solicitor, nor must he use his position as a solicitor to take unfair advantage either for himself or another person.
(2) A solicitor must act towards other solicitors with complete frankness and good faith consistent with the overriding duty to his client.

Breach of these rules renders the solicitor liable to disciplinary action.

Do not attempt to mislead the other side by concealing amendments you have made to their draft, for example by writing a covering letter which draws attention to some amendments and not to others. Any deliberate attempt to mislead could be criminally fraudulent as well as amounting to professional misconduct.

Do not attempt to take advantage of a mistake made by the other side. Point it out to them. They may otherwise be able to claim rectification of the document to incorporate an omitted provision or allege that the agreement is a nullity, so enabling them to resist specific performance.

1.6 FURTHER READING

Melville *Draftsman's Handbook* (Longman, 1991)
Robinson *Drafting* (Butterworth, 1980)
Berg *Drafting Commercial Agreements* (Butterworth, 1991)
Piesse and Aitken *The Elements of Drafting* (Law Book Company, 1991)
Gowers *The Complete Plain Words* (Penguin, 1987)
Fowlers *Modern English Usage* (Oxford University Press, 1983)
Adler *Clarity for Lawyers* (The Law Society, 1990)
National Consumer Council *Plain English for Lawyers* (1990)

PART II

LEGAL RESEARCH

Chapter 2

INTRODUCTION TO LEGAL RESEARCH

Chapter 2 contents

2.1 THE OBJECT OF THIS PART

The legal research Part of this Resource Book takes as its focus the inevitable moment, which will probably arise within one month of a trainee's arrival at his firm, when his principal asks him to check a point of law. The academic stage of legal education will have introduced the trainee to legal research and the use of a law library but now, for the first time, he will be handling a problem which concerns a real client, and which tests his own competence as a practising lawyer.

In relation to legal research, this book aims to build on existing academic skills and to offer an introduction to research in practice. The most obvious difference between academic and practical research derives from the aim of the research. Most academic research will be directed to achieving a general understanding of one subject or topic. Practical research benefits from such an understanding, but it is usually more limited. Its aim is to find a solution to a specific problem of a particular client. This book focuses on practical research.

At the highest level, practical research is complex. For example, advising a client on the correct structure for a company takeover will involve the analysis of a considerable amount of factual information, familiarity with a range of areas of law, and sensitivity to the practical implications of each possible course of action. It is reasonable to assume, however, that the trainee will not be required to begin at this level. He can expect to start by researching under supervision, in a defined area of practice, with tasks which do not stretch his capacity unduly. This Resource Book follows these assumptions. It does not offer a model of legal research which will last for life. Instead, it offers the trainee the opportunity to adapt his academic skills to the requirements of practice before deploying them in the real world.

2.2 ELEMENTS OF LEGAL RESEARCH

Practical legal research aims at solving a specific problem for a particular client. It can be analysed as involving four separate elements.

2.2.1 Assembling the facts

Legal research cannot begin until the facts of the case have been assembled and understood. This will involve taking full instructions from a client, and is dependent on the separate skill of interviewing. It is also dependent on legal analysis which will determine the facts of the case which are material. Legal analysis may require investigation of some specific facts. For example, if the client is seeking a divorce, he will be asked questions linked to the five possible methods of establishing grounds for the divorce. In addition, extensive factual research may be required, for instance in personal injury litigation where it may take time to determine the extent and nature of the injury. In any event, where evidence is doubtful, the factual context of the research will be uncertain, and it may be necessary to base the research on a range of possible factual situations.

2.2.2 Legal analysis

Legal analysis is a core skill of a lawyer. For a solicitor, it is the process by which the client's rights are defined by reference to legal authority and principle. The techniques of analysis vary with the subject-matter. The analytical skills required in company law are quite different from those required in criminal litigation. Training in legal method may form part of an introduction to the academic stage of legal education, but after that the student becomes a lawyer by exploring the concepts of separate divisions of the law, step by step. This has implications for the objectives and structure of the legal research section of this book, which are explained below (see **2.3**).

2.2.3 Library skills

After preliminary legal analysis of a problem, the next stage usually involves use of the law library, in two possible ways.

(1) It may be necessary to check the law to confirm or extend the preliminary analysis. This will usually involve use of practitioner texts.
(2) It may be necessary to trace the primary sources for a point of law in order to provide an authority which could be cited in court. This may involve updating, ie checking that the authority has not been superseded.

Clearly, these exercises may show that the preliminary analysis was wrong, in which case the process must be repeated.

2.2.4 Applying the results

The last stage of the research process is its application to the client's problem. Advice to the client is not, of itself, one of the elements of research, but clearly the product of research must be formulated in such a way that it can form the basis of advice. It must be tailored to the needs of the client. Where the researcher is not the adviser, for example where a trainee carries out research for his principal, it will be necessary to provide a clear report which can form the basis of the advice given to the client.

2.3 SCOPE OF THE RESOURCE BOOK

From the above, it should be apparent that there are difficulties in developing legal research as an independent skill. Any model for performance of the skill might be too abstract to be useful, because the core element of legal analysis is best developed in the context of particular areas of the law.

This Resource Book assumes that problem-solving as a whole is best dealt with in the context of particular subjects, but aims to provide an introduction to cover the elements which can be isolated from their context. Library skills can sensibly be dealt with in this way, if two assumptions are made. The first is that the trainee will not have full responsibility, initially, for handling the matter researched. Instead, his principal will take responsibility for assembling the facts, and preliminary legal analysis. The trainee's responsibility is assumed to be limited to checking the law, tracing primary sources, and reporting the results. The second assumption is that the trainee should concentrate, initially, on general sources, rather than those which concern only a particular branch of the law, for example becoming familiar with use of *Current Law* before looking at *Simon's Tax Intelligence*.

2.4 LIBRARY SKILLS: OBJECTIVES

2.4.1 Criteria of effective research

To demonstrate competence in library skills the trainee must find and report the relevant material in the quickest possible time. This involves:

(1) organising the research;
(2) identifying the correct sources;
(3) recording the research;
(4) extracting the key points;
(5) reporting the results clearly in a form which will be of use to the adviser.

2.4.2 Methods of effective research

There is no mechanical formula which will enable the trainee to do all this, but the following general points should be borne in mind.

Organising the research

Before starting, formulate a research plan. Analyse the problem. Does it involve a single issue, or a number of issues? Will different research materials be relevant to different parts of the problem? Which sources are most likely to provide an answer? Will an answer from a practitioner textbook be adequate, or is it necessary to look at primary sources? How likely is it that there have been recent changes in the law? What are the likely subject headings under which the problem might be classified? If the trainee considers these questions first, he will be able to plan his research more effectively.

Identifying the correct sources

The ability to identify the correct sources depends on thorough familiarity with the sources available, and the following sections of the Resource Book deal with this. The usual procedure will be to begin by looking at a commentary on the law, a textbook, or a general work such as *Halsbury's Laws of England*. This should direct the trainee to a primary source, such as case-law, statute, or delegated legislation. These primary sources are authoritative, and should be checked carefully. Once the primary source has been found, an updating exercise should be performed as a matter of routine to check that the authority remains effective. Textbooks can be wrong.

Recording the research

Record the sources used and the information found. It may be that the relevance of material is only realised at the end of the research. If a record has been kept, it is possible to check back quickly without duplication of effort.

Extracting the key points

The adviser will not thank the researcher if he reports his research by producing armfuls of law reports and statutes. A written report should be produced which extracts the relevant information from the source material. The report should be a summary of material extracted as the research proceeds. This will involve the essential academic skills of interpretation of statutes and case analysis.

Reporting the results clearly

The final report of the research must be intelligible to the adviser and capable of forming the basis for advice. The ability to draft a report depends on a trainee's written communication skills (see Chapter 1). However, this legal research section ends with some specific points on communication between researcher and adviser.

2.5 PROBLEM-SOLVING: CRITERIA OF EFFECTIVE RESEARCH

In relation to problem-solving as a whole, a wider test of competence is required. In addition to criteria listed at **2.4.1**, this involves:

(1) in the light of the client's objectives:
   (a) identifying the material facts of his current position; and
   (b) correctly analysing the legal issues raised;

(2) according to context, identifying the legal procedure, or argument, or (in the context of drafting) form of words which can be used to meet the client's objectives.

Chapter 3

CHECKING THE LAW

3.1 INTRODUCTION

The assumption to be made, for our present purposes, when dealing with library skills is that the principal has already completed an analysis of the relevant facts and made a preliminary legal analysis. The trainee's task is then to check the law so that he may confirm or alter his principal's preliminary legal analysis. When this is done, the trainee will look at primary sources to give final authority to that analysis.

Assume that the trainee has identified the legal issues. He cannot normally begin his research by referring to primary sources. Even if his knowledge of the law in the particular area is substantial, it is normally wiser to begin the research by referring to a general statement of the law relating to the relevant issues, so as to gain a comprehensive overview of the applicable law. Ideally, such a general statement would be concise, yet comprehensive, dealing with points of fine detail, perhaps in appendices or footnotes, and containing detailed references to primary sources.

Such a general statement of the law is to be found in legal encyclopedias and practitioner textbooks. The first step is to check to see if there is an available practitioner textbook which covers the relevant area. If not, the trainee should consult a legal encyclopedia, such as *Halsbury's Laws of England*, which gives an up-to-date coverage of the whole of the law of England and Wales. Either source should have an updating system, which should be used at this stage, as it is clearly important that the trainee's initial view of the law be as recent as possible. (The topic of updating is dealt with in detail in Chapter 5, since the trainee must always check that his research is valid as at the date of his report.)

3.2 PRACTITIONER TEXTBOOKS

General books

The trainee is probably more familiar with student textbooks than with practitioner works. In the office, the trainee would not normally refer to student textbooks or other academic works, since their treatment of the subject would not necessarily assist a quick and practical assessment of the law relating to the issues. Furthermore, the practitioner textbook is likely to be extremely comprehensive and will also have the benefit of a detailed index.

The trainee must check that the statement of law which he finds is as up to date as possible. Publishers make various arrangements to keep such works up to date, and the trainee must ensure that he understands how this is done in any book which he uses. Publishers do not necessarily issue a new edition of a work each year (although this may occur in some subjects such as revenue law in which there are inevitably many changes of law each year and where an annual edition is justified).

The preface to the work will normally state the date up to which the law is correct. The trainee should then check to see if a supplement has been published. Supplements are usually published annually and on a cumulative basis, so that earlier supplements need not be retained. Supplements are usually in paperback form.

A useful alternative to the updating problem is the loose-leaf system. Here the work is updated several times each year by the issue of supplements or 'Service Packs' containing new pages, with instructions for insertion of the new pages and removal of out-of-date pages. This is better than the use of an updating supplement where the researcher usually needs to search the supplement by means of a 'key' which will show whether a given page or paragraph number of the textbook is referred to in the supplement. In the loose-leaf system, changes in the law can be integrated into the main work itself. Furthermore, the greater frequency of issue of updating packs usually means that the loose-leaf work is more up to date than the textbook with its annual cumulative supplement. However, the trainee must check that all supplements to a loose-leaf work have been filed. This can be done very quickly by checking the filing record kept in the book.

Practice books

Apart from practitioner textbooks which deal with specific areas of the law, practitioners make use of specialised 'practice books'. In litigation, examples are:

The Supreme Court Practice ('The White Book')
The County Court Practice ('The Green Book')
Archbold's Pleadings, Evidence and Practice in Criminal Cases
Stone's Justices' Manual.

Precedent books

Mention should also be made of the precedent books which are available to the practitioner, although these would not normally be relevant to the trainee conducting legal research. They are used by practitioners to assist in the drafting of documents by giving examples of wording which can be adapted or adopted for use in a given matter.

3.3 *HALSBURY'S LAWS OF ENGLAND*

Halsbury's Laws of England is an encyclopedia which is now in its fourth edition, completed in 1986. The trainee should read the separate User's Guide which is supplied with the main volumes.

A search in *Halsbury's Laws* usually involves use of:

(1) the Consolidated Index;
(2) the main volumes;
(3) the annual Cumulative Supplement;
(4) the Current Service.

3.3.1 The Consolidated Index

It has been assumed that the trainee has identified the legal issues which lie at the heart of the problem. It is crucial, now, to pick the word which is most likely to be used in an index to find the relevant statement of the law. This sounds obvious and yet proper use of an index is a skill in itself. The trainee must accept that, if his original search word is unproductive, a better alternative must be found. A successful search in the Consolidated Index will produce both the relevant main volume number and a paragraph number. The index does not give the relevant page number. If the paragraph number is followed by the letter 'n' with a small superscript number, this is a reference to a footnote to the paragraph which may refer to case-law and statutory or other sources.

3.3.2 The main volumes

There are 52 main volumes, arranged alphabetically according to subject titles. Use of the Consolidated Index ensures that the trainee refers to the appropriate main volume, although in a straightforward case, where the issue and subject matter are clear-cut, he could simply go to the relevant main volume and use its own index.

3.3.3 The annual Cumulative Supplement

The information contained in a main volume may be out of date. At this stage, reference should be made to the most recent annual Cumulative Supplement. Check the supplement by referring to the main volume number and the paragraph number in that main volume.

3.3.4 The Current Service

To check that there has been no change in the law since the date of the latest Cumulative Supplement, the trainee must now refer to the loose-leaf Current Service, published monthly. This contains a 'noter-up', which uses the same order of material as in the supplement, and refers to developments in the law since the publication of the most recent supplement. In addition, the service contains a Monthly Review which deals with developments since the last supplement but which can be read on its own as a monthly digest. This is cross-referenced to the main work by the Cumulative Index to the Monthly Reviews. (The contents of the Monthly Reviews, in a summarised form, appear in the Annual Abridgement which shows the major areas of change in law over a particular year.)

This important subject of updating is referred to in greater detail in Chapter 5.

3.3.5 Volumes 51 and 52

Main volumes 51 and 52 are concerned with aspects of European Community law which are relevant to English law. The index to both volumes is contained in Volume 52.

Chapter 4

USING PRIMARY SOURCES

Chapter 4 contents
Legislative materials
Judicial decisions

4.1 LEGISLATIVE MATERIALS

4.1.1 Introduction

This section is concerned with the efficient identification, location and reading of legislative materials: statutes, subordinate legislation and statute-related rules.

4.1.2 UK statutes citation

The citation of statutes has varied throughout history. A number of citations may be given in respect of a single statute. The following is a short guide which will help to locate, in particular, older statutes.

1215–1548

Statutes for the period 1215–1548 are not cited individually but by the name of the place where Parliament sat at the time. All legislation passed in one session is a 'statute'. Each individual 'Act' forms a separate chapter (abbreviated to 'ch' or 'c') but has no separate title. Today, an accompanying reference is usually given referring to the monarch and regnal year.

Example
'Statute of Gloucester 1278 6 Edw. 1, c.5' refers to an Act relating to tenancies and dilapidation.

1548–1963

From 1548 onwards, Acts are cited individually by reference to the Parliamentary session when they received Royal Assent, and by the regnal year.

A list of the regnal years and the corresponding calendar years can be found in Sweet & Maxwell's *Guide to Law Reports and Statutes*.

Often, an alternative 'short title' reference will be given. This is either in the Act itself ('this Act may be cited as . . .') or provided for in a Short Titles Act.

Example
'7 Wm IV and 1 Vict., c. 26' is the Wills Act 1837.

Modern citations

The system of reference to regnal years was abolished with effect from 1 January 1963.

Example
'Justices of the Peace Act 1979, c.55', which is more usually referred to simply as the Justices of the Peace Act 1979.

Incomplete citations

Most statutes can be identified even from an incomplete citation (see **4.1.3**). If a full citation is required, it can be found from several sources depending on the initial information. Always try the most obvious source first: a textbook, or practitioner work if the subject area is known. Other sources are:

TITLE ONLY
Halsbury's Statutes has a Table of Statutes and General Index with an alphabetical list of all statutes passed. The most recent Current Law Legislation Citator has an alphabetical list of all post-1947 statutes and also pre-1947 statutes affected since that date (eg by repeal or case reference).

APPROXIMATE YEAR, INCOMPLETE TITLE
Halsbury's Table of Statutes and General Index has a chronological list of statutes (in addition to *Halsbury's* two-volume Chronological Tables).

SUBJECT AREA ONLY
The relevant subject volume of *Halsbury's Statutes* (or a practitioner work) can be checked. Use *Halsbury's Statutes* Noter-up Service for more recent statutes.

4.1.3 Finding a statute

There are several ways to locate the text of a statute. The sources most readily available in practice are listed below. Remember, the text may have been amended and this must be checked.

Practitioner works

Practitioner works may contain the text, together with annotations, of relevant statutes. Also, they often contain subordinate legislation. For example, Palmer's *Company Law*, Volume 3 contains the texts of company law statutes and statutory instruments, and Practice Directions of the Companies Court.

Many of these works are in loose-leaf form, and updated material is issued by the publishers. Check the latest update and make sure no amendments have been made since that date.

Annotated statutes

There are several texts of annotated statutes arranged either by year or subject. The most widely used annual texts are *Current Law Statutes* (1948–date) and *Butterworths Annotated Legislation Service* (1939–date). Bear in mind that an annual text will not cover any subsequent amendments.

Alternatively, *Halsbury's Statutes* is arranged in bound volumes by subject matter; for example, Treaties of the European Communities: Volume 50.

Halsbury's volumes are updated by reissue but cannot be fully up to date. It is necessary to use the Cumulative Supplement and Noter-up Service (see **5.2.3**). For very recent Acts there is a loose-leaf Current Statutes Service. Repealed Acts or sections will not be reproduced when the volumes are reissued, but there will be a note of any repeal or amendment.

Halsbury's Statutes is initially accessed by consulting the latest volume of the Table of Statutes and General Index which contains both alphabetical and chronological lists of statutes. It also contains separate subject indexes to the main volumes and the Current Service. (For updating procedure see **5.2.3**.)

Other sources

Statutes of the Realm (1235–1713)
Statutes at Large (1225–1869)
Public General Acts and Measures (1831–date)
Law Reports: Statutes (1866–date)

Official copies

Official copies of Acts can be purchased from HMSO. This is useful when the text of a very recent Act is required. The publication of new Acts is reported in the *Daily List* of parliamentary publications, which also lists the commencement date of each statute.

Is it in force?

Check for any commencement section in the statute. If there is none, the Act comes into force on the day of the Royal Assent. This date is in square brackets after the long title.

Example
Time Share Act 1992

1992 CHAPTER 35

An Act to provide for rights to cancel certain agreements about time-share accommodation. [16 March 1992]

A commencement section may state a specific date or a 'day or days to be appointed'. Different sections of the Act may come into force on different days. A statutory instrument will be issued, usually bearing the title of the statute followed by '(Commencement) Order'. If several commencement orders have been issued they will be numbered. For example:

> Companies Act 1989 '(Commencement No 3) Order 1990'.

To check commencement, see the latest volume of *Is it in Force?* which provides a chronological list of post-1966 statutes and commencement dates. The Noter-up Service must also be checked and, after the noter-up date, check *Current Law* (see **5.2.1**) and the *Daily List* of parliamentary publications, issued by HMSO.

Halsbury's Statutes also notes the commencement dates of all statutes up to the volume date. This is useful for pre-1966 statutes or when *Is it in Force?* is unavailable.

Halsbury's Statutory Instruments service contains an alphabetical list of recent commencement orders.

Legal periodicals also note new commencement orders, but these are not necessarily comprehensive.

LEXIS provides a comprehensive updating service (see **7.2.2**).

4.1.4 Delegated (or subordinate) legislation

Delegated legislation is legislation made by a person or body other than Parliament. Generally, the authority for this lies in the 'parent' Act.

Examples are regulations, orders and procedural rules.

Validity

Delegated legislation should be within the scope of the authority conferred (intra vires). If not, it can be challenged as being ultra vires.

Forms

Delegated legislation is generally made by statutory instrument and published by HMSO.

Local authorities may have made by-laws. Copies of these are obtainable from them, for a fee.

Statutory instruments

To understand the terminology used in a statutory instrument (SI), it is useful to know something of the normal procedure for making them.

The relevant Minister 'makes' the regulation or order (ie it is drafted by a civil servant) and 'lays' it before Parliament. The instrument will state (after the title) the date when made, laid and, normally, when it comes into force, although the date may be contained in the body of the instrument. The instrument often has an explanatory note at the end of it which can provide useful cross-references.

CITATION

Statutory instruments are cited by year followed by numerical reference, for example: SI 1992/1758.

FINDING A STATUTORY INSTRUMENT

There is a vast number of statutory instruments. Official texts are published by HMSO both separately and in annual volumes. Few libraries keep these, most rely on *Halsbury's Statutory Instruments*. This hardback set of volumes is arranged alphabetically by subject matter and lists all SIs in force. It prints the full texts of selected SIs and summarises the rest. It is initially accessed via the Consolidated Index which is revised annually. There is a User's Guide to *Halsbury's Statutory Instruments*.

The two-volume looseleaf service updates and cross-references the system. (For updating procedure see **5.2.4**.)

Volume 1 contains a chronological list of all instruments referred to in the main volumes. This is useful if the SI number is known but the subject matter is unclear. The statute table could also be used to check the subject head if the title of the enabling Act is known.

The annual Cumulative Supplement and Monthly Survey Key notes up any changes by subject matter. It may refer to 'Additional texts' which are copies of more recent SIs to be found in Volume 2 of the Service. A Monthly Survey summarises recent SIs chronologically.

For even more recent SIs or amendments the *Current Law Monthly Digest* will need to be checked. Very recent SIs will be noted in the *Daily List* of parliamentary publications from HMSO. Individual copies of the text would have to be purchased from HMSO.

The texts of SIs can also be found in practitioner works. For example, The Rules of the Supreme Court are reproduced in the White Book, the County Court Rules in the Green Book, and both are included in various encyclopedias.

LEXIS has the full texts of current statutory instruments (see **7.2.2**).

4.1.5 Statute-related rules

Statute-related rules may be materials not enacted as legislation but of importance to it, such as circulars issued by Ministers on green belt policies in planning law.

These circulars, guidelines, etc may be published by and obtained from HMSO or the government department. Practitioner works may also contain them.

4.1.6 EC legislation

UK legislation has to be read in conjunction with any relevant EC law (see Chapter 6).

4.1.7 Understanding legislative materials

The most important rule is to read the material as a whole. This means not only all the legislative materials but any case-law as well. The source material containing the text of the statute or statutory instrument, eg textbooks, practitioner works or *Halsbury's Statutes*, may refer to relevant case-law. Check each source date and update further from that, if necessary.

One useful method of ensuring that the most up-to-date material is considered is to use the most recent *Current Law Year Book* together with the Monthly Digests (see Chapter 5). Note that the entries under subject headings refer to any development on a statute (whether by statute, statutory instrument or case-law). The Cumulative Index will refer to paragraphs in the relevant *Year Book* or Digest which should be consulted.

If you know that there is a reported case (or cases) on a statutory provision (and roughly the period), a quick check in the Index to the Law Reports may help. The volumes cover various periods (1981–1990 cumulative, 1991 separate) and cross-reference all cases reported in the major reports which considered any statutory provision (including statutory instruments). Look at the sections 'Statutes (or Statutory Instruments) Judicially Considered' which refers to each statute chronologically. An update would still be needed via the *Current Law* Monthly Digest.

If a check is to be made on the interpretation of a particular word or phrase, cases can be checked, again using *Current Law*. *Stroud's Judicial Dictionary* is easy to use for individual words but again needs updating to ensure accuracy. *Words and Phrases Legally Defined* may also be useful.

Halsbury's Laws, Volume 44, Statutes, contains a useful summary of the rules of interpretation and construction, including definitions of certain words and phrases used in statutes.

4.2 JUDICIAL DECISIONS

There are numerous sources for a report of a case. The most readily available sources are summarised below.

4.2.1 Law reports

The Law Reports (1865–date)

In 1865, a Council of Law Reporting was set up to publish reports of important cases. In 1870, it became the 'Incorporated Council of Law Reporting for England and Wales'. The Council, which is controlled by the Inns of Court and the Law Society, produces reports known simply as *The Law Reports.*

The Law Reports are the official set of case reports. In each case report, counsel's argument is summarised and the judgment is revised by the judge before publication. The Law Report reference is cited in preference to other reports.

A table of the modes of citation of these reports appears at the end of this chapter.

The Weekly Law Reports

Since 1953, the Council has also published *The Weekly Law Reports* ('the Weeklies'). In these case reports, counsel's arguments are not summarised and the judgments are not revised before publication.

Three volumes are published each year. Volume 1 – Less important cases, not intended for republication in *The Law Reports.* This will include cases likely to go to appeal. Volumes 2 and 3 – Cases likely to be published in *The Law Reports,* set out chronologically.

The Weeklies are first published in paperback and republished, cumulated, in hardback at the end of the year.

Citation: *Wooldridge v Summer* [1962] 3 WLR 616.

The All England Law Reports

The All England Law Reports are a well-known and very reliable series of general reports. They are published weekly in paperback and republished, cumulated, in hardback at the end of each year. Like the Weeklies, counsel's arguments are omitted and judgments are not revised. There are usually two or three volumes for each year, set out chronologically.

Citation: *R v Kelly* [1965] 2 All ER 250.

Specialist reports

There are numerous specialist reports including:
Criminal Appeal Reports (Cr App Rep)
Tax Cases (TC)
Road Traffic Reports (RTR)
Family Law Reports (FLR)
Industrial Tribunal Reports (ITR)
Estates Gazette Law Reports (EGLR).

Legal periodicals

Many legal periodicals contain law reports including:
Solicitors' Journal (Sol Jo), New Law Journal (NLJ) and Criminal Law Review (CrimLR) .

Newspapers

The Times and *The Independent*, for example, contain daily law reports.

Many law reports are cited by use of abbreviations. Most modern abbreviations can be found in *Current Law* (Monthly Digests, Year Books and Citators) *Halsbury's Laws*, Volume 1 and the first volume to the Digest of Cases.

4.2.2 Incomplete citations

By name only

A researcher may know the name of the case but not its citation (or the researcher may need alternative citations to find an accessible report). Where the subject-matter is known, a check of the name in a textbook or practitioner book may give the researcher the reference straightaway.

If this is unsuccessful or the subject matter is not known, the *Current Law* Case Citator is useful. This contains an alphabetical list of cases (of any date) referred to in reported cases from 1947 onwards. Several references may be given. The citator will also note if this case was followed, distinguished or applied in subsequent cases. If the case is likely to be recent, check the Monthly Digest.

For old cases, *The Law Reports* Index to the Digest of Cases could be used. It covers the period 1865–1950.

Other possible sources are the indexes to the major reports. The *Current Law* Citator should have these but, especially with recent cases, the citations may not yet have appeared in *Current Law*. The Daily Law Reports index is up to date to within a fortnight.

A check could also be made in *Halsbury's Laws* in the index to the relevant subject volume.

If this fails, a LEXIS search might reveal an unreported decision.

By subject matter only

Where the general nature of the case is known but not its name, a case can be found easily if the approximate year is known. The *Current Law* Year Books have brief summaries of cases reported that year listed under subject headings. For recent cases, check the subject heading in the latest Monthly Digest. If there is no information on year or name, tracing a case by subject matter alone is very time-consuming unless a computer-based system such as LEXIS is used. Therefore, recheck to see if there is any further information (eg era of the case). If not, a search will have to be made using the Digest to the Law Reports (1865–1950) and the Index (1951–date) under the relevant subject head.

Note on case names

Although most cases are named in the form of *Smith v Jones*, it is worth being familiar with the other forms of case name. First, it helps for checking entries in tables and indexes. Secondly, it can throw light on the subject area and date of the case.

Smith v Jones

This is the usual form in civil cases, ie Plaintiff v Defendant (Pursuer v Defender in Scottish cases), or Appellant v Respondent. (However, this form could also refer to a criminal case in the magistrate's court, where the report is likely to be of an appeal to the Queen's Bench Divisional Court.)

R v Store (or Rex or Reg)
This is the usual form in criminal cases commencing in the Crown Court.

R v Secretary of State for the Home Department, ex parte Black
This is the usual form of name for cases in the Divisional Court of the Queen's Bench Division by way of judicial review (as here) or by way of case stated from a magistrates' court or Crown Court (in which case the name of the court will be given as defendant). The name given after the words 'ex parte' is that of the applicant, and as these cases are often known by that name, most (but not all) indexes provide cross-references from it.

Ex parte White
This form of name is usually where the report is on a point raised only at an ex parte hearing of one party, and the case does not proceed to trial between the parties; typically, nowadays, cases on application for leave to apply for judicial review.

Attorney-General, ex relator Green v Sarum Borough Council
This is the form for a relator action to obtain relief in public law matters through the Attorney-General (likely to be pre-1977).

Re Boggis
Re Boggis, *In the goods of Boggis*, *Re Boggis Will Trusts* and *In the estate of Boggis* are used in wills and probate cases where the name cited is that of the deceased (although the executors or administrators brought the case before the court).

Re a company No 00034607 of 1990
This is likely to be a company insolvency case.

Re S (A Minor) (Care Proceedings: Wardship Summons)
In family law cases, the full name of the minor cannot be given. The modern practice is to give the subject-matter of the case in parenthesis to help distinguish it from others.

Practice Direction (Family Court: Wardship Summonses)
Practice Directions are not case reports as such, but are published in the law reports. There are also Practice Notes, Practice Statements and, from the House of Lords, Procedure Directions.

The Hispaniola
This citation uses the name of a ship in a shipping case.

4.2.3 Understanding case reports

The following notes are an essential guide to matters to bear in mind when reading a case report.

General layout of law reports

COURT
TITLE OF CASE

Date of Judgment JUDGES

1 Summary
2 Headnote
3 Argument
4 Judgment
5 Order
6 Parties' representatives
7 Reporter

Court

The status of the court may be significant, bearing in mind the doctrine of precedent (stare decisis) which generally requires that English courts are bound to follow decisions made in earlier cases.

Previous cases may be cited in argument. These will appear in the report, normally after the headnote. There will usually be a list of cases referred to by the judges, again after the headnote.

If the case is recent, the status of the court may alert the researcher to the possibility of appeal. If an appeal is likely, check the date of the judgment and update from that date (which may differ considerably from the time the decision was reported).

Summary and headnote

The summary is useful to find out the legal points of the case and the relevant statutory provisions. This type of summary may be used for cross-referencing purposes in the subject indexes. The headnote provides a summary of the essential facts of the case, the law, the decision and order (or orders) of the court. As the headnote is, however, the reporter's interpretation of the case, it may not always be accurate and a full reading of the case is always advisable, where time permits.

Argument

Argument of the parties' representatives is usually only reported in *The Law Reports*.

Judgment

A judgment should follow the general order of: statements of fact, statements of law and, finally, application of law to material (ie legally relevant) facts. This order should enable the lawyer to distinguish, where necessary, the ratio decidendi from obiter dictum (or dicta) in the judgment. However, not all judgments will follow this order. The headnote can, with care, be used to find the ratio (or rationes).

Orders

It may be important to check the type of order (or orders) finally granted by the court. Sometimes the report may give useful guidance on the format to be adopted for certain types of orders.

Parties' representatives

Occasionally it can be useful to know which counsel and solicitors were involved in a case.

4.2.4 The table of the Law Reports

The mode of citation is given in brackets. In the first, second and third columns, dots (. . .) are put where the number of the volume would appear in the citation. In the fourth column, square brackets ([ ]) are put where the year would appear in the citation.

<table>
<tr><th>1866–1875</th><th>1875–1880</th><th>1881–1890</th><th>1891–present</th></tr>
<tr><td>House of Lords, English and Irish Appeals (LR . . . HL)</td><td rowspan="3">Appeal Cases (. . . App Cas)</td><td rowspan="3">Appeal Cases (. . . App Cas)</td><td rowspan="3">Appeal Cases ([ ] AC)</td></tr>
<tr><td>House of Lords, Scots and Divorce Appeals (LR . . . HLSc or LR . . . HLSc and Div)</td></tr>
<tr><td>Privy Council Appeals (LR . . . PC)</td></tr>
<tr><td>Chancery Appeal Cases (LR . . . Ch or Ch App)</td><td rowspan="2">Chancery Division (. . . Ch D)</td><td rowspan="2">Chancery Division (. . . Ch D)</td><td rowspan="2">Chancery Division ([ ] Ch)</td></tr>
<tr><td>Equity Cases (LR . . . Eq)</td></tr>
<tr><td>Queen's Bench Cases (LR . . . QB)</td><td rowspan="2">Queen's Bench Division (. . . QBD)</td><td rowspan="4">Queen's Bench Division (. . . QBD)</td><td rowspan="4">Queen's (or King's) Bench Division ([ ] QB or KB) etc.</td></tr>
<tr><td>Crown Cases Reserved (LR CC or . . . CCR)</td></tr>
<tr><td>Common Pleas Cases (LR. . . CP)</td><td>Common Pleas Division (. . . CPD)</td></tr>
<tr><td>Exchequer Cases (LR . . . Ex)</td><td>Exchequer Division (. . . Ex D)</td></tr>
<tr><td>Admiralty and Ecclesiastical Cases (LR . . . A & E)</td><td rowspan="2">Probate Division (. . . PD)</td><td rowspan="2">Probate Division (. . . PD)</td><td rowspan="2">Probate Division ([ ] P) Since 1972 Family Division ([ ] Fam)</td></tr>
<tr><td>Probate and Divorce Cases (LR . . . P & D)</td></tr>
</table>

Chapter 5

UPDATING

Chapter 5 contents
Introduction
Standard updating sources
Very recent developments

5.1 INTRODUCTION

5.1.1 A routine exercise

Developments occur even in the more sluggish backwaters of the law, and the practitioner must keep up to date. Updating research should therefore be a matter of routine, performed even where use of the sources of first resort seems to have produced a satisfactory answer. Here, as elsewhere, the essence of the skill of research is to be meticulous.

5.1.2 Likely developments

When updating, the researcher should work out what developments are most likely to have occurred. He can then begin by checking for these. Is the area one which generates a large volume of case-law, affecting earlier cases, or the interpretation of a statute? Is it an area where the law can be changed by statutory instrument? Is it likely that new legislation has been enacted? Thorough updating will check for all these things, but the efficient researcher will check the most likely developments first.

5.1.3 General procedure

The particular procedure for updating will vary with the source used, but the following general points should be borne in mind.

(1) Begin by noting the information which is to be updated, with full references.
(2) In particular, note the date of the edition or issue in which the information was found.
(3) Stay with the source in which you found that information until it ceases to prove useful. For instance, if information has been found in a textbook, check whether any supplement has been issued.
(4) Check the date of information in any more recent source used.
(5) When switching sources, always check the database of the new source which may provide a different range of information from other sources used. If unfamiliar with its use, look for a user's guide, or a preface containing an explanation.
(6) Make notes of information and references during the investigation.

5.2 STANDARD UPDATING SOURCES

5.2.1 *Current Law*

What is Current Law?

Current Law is the most general updating source available. It consists of the *Current Law* Citators, the Monthly Digest, and the Year Books (which consolidate the Monthly Digest). *Current Law Statutes Annotated* is a separate, self-contained service.

The Current Law Citators

The *Current Law* Citators can be used to check post-1947 developments. There is a Case Citator, and a separate Legislation Citator.

THE CASE CITATOR

The use of the Case Citator to find the citation of a case and to check how it has been dealt with in later cases is described in **4.2.2**. There are three volumes (1948–76, 1977–88, 1989–date). Updating procedure involves finding the volume in which the case is first noted, and then checking the case lists in later volumes for subsequent developments. The Citator gives the paragraph in the Year Book where the development is reported.

THE LEGISLATION CITATOR

The use of the Legislation Citator to find a statute is described in **4.1.2**. It can also be used to check for amendments, repeals, and cases interpreting the statute. Again, there are three volumes. Updating procedure involves finding the volume where the statute is first noted. It will be found listed in chronological order, with separate notes on each section. The later volumes must also be checked for subsequent developments.

The Monthly Digest

The Monthly Digest can be used in a number of different ways:

UPDATING THE CASE CITATOR

The final stage in tracing the history of a case will be to check the Cumulative Table of Cases in the Monthly Digest covering the years not covered in the latest Case Citator. The Digests are cumulative for each year, so it is only necessary to check the December issue for a completed year, and the latest issue for the current year. The entry will refer to the note number and edition of the Monthly Digest in which the development was reported.

UPDATING THE LEGISLATION CITATOR

The final stage in checking legislative developments will be to check the Statute Citator in the Monthly Digests for the years not covered by the latest Legislation Citator. These are cumulative for each year.

The procedure for checking is as follows:

(1) note the title, regnal year and chapter of the Act in question, and the section or schedule being checked;
(2) check the statute citator in the latest Monthly Digest for an entry identified by the reference in (1);
(3) for the text of the development, use other sources. A note on the development may be found in the Monthly Digests. This can be accessed by using the Case Table, alphabetical list of SIs, or subject index, as appropriate.

Checking recent developments by subject heading

Some recent developments may not be reported as developments of earlier cases or statutes. Updating is only complete if the researcher checks for such developments by using the Cumulative Subject Index in *Current Law*. The procedure here is as follows:

(1) find the latest issue of the Monthly Digest;
(2) check the list of subject headings at the beginning, and identify the heading to be researched;
(3) turn to the Cumulative Index. Check under the heading identified in (2) for any reference to the topic to be researched;
(4) check the December issue for the previous year, or the Year Book if published, using the same method. Always check the headings in use for the particular volume;
(5) check earlier Year Books if necessary.

Other uses

The Monthly Digest also contains up-to-date information on quantum of damages for personal injuries, words and phrases judicially considered, High Court fees, progress of Bills in Parliament, and dates of commencement of statutes.

5.2.2 *Halsbury's Laws*

Updating via Halsbury's Laws

Updating by using *Halsbury's Laws* is appropriate where the main volumes of *Halsbury's Laws* have already been used, and relevant material has been found.

The procedure here is as follows:

(1) make a note of the edition, volume, title, paragraph and note number where the relevant information was found;
(2) find the latest Cumulative Supplement. This is issued annually, and updates the main work to 31 October each year;
(3) check the Cumulative Supplement for any entry identified by the reference in (1) above;
(4) find the loose-leaf Current Service Volume. This will update for developments since 31 October of the previous year;
(5) check the Noter-up in the Current Service Volume, for any entry identified by the reference in (1) above;
(6) if an entry is found, further detail will be found in the Monthly Reviews in the Current Service Volume. This can be accessed by using the Cumulative Index. The Noter-up gives a reference to a case, statute or statutory instrument. The Cumulative Index will identify which paragraph of the Monthly Reviews deals with the item.

General updating

The Cumulative Supplement and Current Service can be used directly without first using the main work by use of the subject indexes. This would be appropriate where the researcher knew of a recent development which would not be noted in the main work.

In addition, the Current Service provides sections covering recent material, inter alia, on commencement of statutes, personal injuries litigation, and interpretation of words and phrases.

A separate publication which may be used for updating is the Annual Abridgment. This covers the same material as the Current Service, but is published in hardback, and presents the developments for each calendar year. It may be useful if the researcher knows the year in which a development occurred.

5.2.3 *Halsbury's Statutes*

Updating references in the main work

The standard procedures for using *Halsbury's Statutes* will alert the researcher to the existence of statutes up to the date of issue of the last Table of Statutes and General Index. This is a single volume issued each August, and contains separate indexes for the main volumes and the Current Service.

Updating involves using the Cumulative Supplement and Noter-up. These will provide information about any developments affecting statutes contained in the main volumes or Current Service, ie cases, statutes or, particularly, statutory instruments.

The procedure is as follows:

(1) from the main volume, or Current Service, note the title of the volume, page number, title of the Act, section, subsection, or Schedule number, or note number, which is to be updated;
(2) find the Cumulative Supplement. This will be up to date to 1 January of the year of the Supplement, but may note later developments;
(3) check the Cumulative Supplement for any entry identified by the reference in (1) above;
(4) find the loose-leaf Noter-up Service. This is normally updated three times a year. Check the date of the latest issue;
(5) check the Noter-up for any entry identified by the reference in (1) above;
(6) to find the text of any statute referred to in the entry, use the Table of Statutes and General Index. Other sources must be used to find the texts of cases or SIs.

Is it in Force?

If any new statute is found in the process of updating, it will be necessary to check whether it has come into effect. The Noter-up Service contains a section which updates the *Is it in Force?* volume of *Halsbury's Statutes*.

5.2.4 *Halsbury's Statutory Instruments*

The use of *Halsbury's Statutory Instruments* to find delegated legislation is described in **4.1.4**. Once the SI has been found, it is then necessary to check for amendments and revocations. The procedure is as follows:

(1) note the title of the SI and the title and number of the volume, and page number where it was found;
(2) find the Annual Supplement in the loose-leaf service (Volume 1) and check it for any entry identified by the reference in (1) above;
(3) find the Monthly Survey Key and Index in the same volume, and check as in (2). The effect of any new SIs listed will be explained in the Monthly Survey Summaries.

5.3 VERY RECENT DEVELOPMENTS

No matter how thorough the research, there will always be a possibility that developments have occurred in the period since the last available information was published. Even with LEXIS or *Current Law*, six weeks may elapse before developments are noted. One approach is to take comfort in the fact that, if all available sources have been checked, no other practitioner is likely to know of a development either.

Possible sources for latest developments are:

(1) the weekly journals including the *New Law Journal*, the *Solicitors Journal* and the *Law Society Gazette* (accessed via the *Legal Journals Index*);
(2) specialist publications in the field in question, for example *Simon's Tax Intelligence*;
(3) for statutory instruments, the *Daily List* of HMSO publications;
(4) daily law reports in the national newspapers (accessed via the *Daily Law Reports Index*).

Chapter 6

EC LAW

6.1 INTRODUCTION

6.1.1 General research

Research into the law of the European Communities is not a task for the faint-hearted. The difficulty of keeping up with the flood of legislation and case-law emanating from Brussels, Luxembourg and Strasbourg is compounded by the fact that much of the material takes a considerable time to filter through the traditional sources. Specialist EC practitioners thus become adept at using all manner of different research methods in their search for proposals which will influence their clients' business decisions: contact with government departments, for instance, may give an instant updating on the development of a particular piece of legislation, thus providing a service which no traditional source can offer.

6.1.2 Library sources

Whilst the importance of entrepreneurial research in the field of EC law cannot be underestimated, the student researcher will first need to be acquainted with the essential library sources. This brief introduction to research into EC law aims to familiarise the student with those sources; after reading this chapter and practising his new skills, the researcher should be able to track down references to EC legislation and case-law and, as a necessary adjunct, begin to develop a feel for spotting the 'Europoint' in a file, even if no such point seems at first sight to be in issue.

It is assumed that the researcher already has a basic knowledge of EC law. Although brief references to certain substantive points of law are inevitable, so far as possible they have been kept to a minimum.

6.2 PRIMARY LEGISLATION

6.2.1 Substance

The primary legislation of European Community Law comprises the following.

(1) The founding treaties which set up the three European Communities (EC). These are:

   (a) the Treaty of Paris 1951, establishing the European Coal and Steel Community (ECSC);
   (b) the Treaty of Rome 1957, establishing the European Atomic Energy Community (EURATOM); and
   (c) the Treaty of Rome 1957, establishing the European Economic Community (EEC).

(2) The treaties and acts which amend the three founding treaties; these include the Brussels Merger Treaty 1965, the Single European Act 1986 and the Maastricht Treaty on European Union 1992.

(3) The accession documents of new Member States, including the 1972 Accession Treaty under which the UK, Denmark and Ireland joined the EC.

6.2.2 Sources of primary legislation

Updated texts of the treaties themselves and the most important of the other primary legislation can be found in:

(1) *Encyclopedia of European Community Law* (Sweet & Maxwell). The volumes marked 'B' contain the primary legislation.
(2) *Halsbury's Statutes* (Butterworths, 4th edn, Vol 50).
(3) *Basic Community Laws* (2nd edn) edited by Rudden and Wyatt (OUPR). The treaties and related primary legislation are contained in Part 1. The second edition does not incorporate the Maastricht Treaty.

6.3 SECONDARY LEGISLATION

6.3.1 Substance

The secondary legislation of the EC comprises acts made by the Council of Ministers and the Commission under the powers granted to them in the treaties (see in particular the EEC Treaty, Articles 189–192).

This legislation has binding force insofar as it consists of:

(1) Regulations, which are binding in their entirety and directly applicable. No further implementation by member states is needed for Regulations to have effect.
(2) Directives, which are binding only as to the result to be achieved but which leave member states a choice of the form and manner of implementation.
(3) Decisions, which are binding in their entirety on the member states or individuals to whom they are addressed.

Alternatively, the legislation may be non-obligatory and take the form of a Recommendation or an Opinion.

6.3.2 Citation of secondary legislation

The researcher's first hurdle in tracing secondary legislation is coming to terms with the rather obscure methods of citation, methods which derive from 1968 when the Official Journal of the EC (see below) was split into two series.

Regulations

Regulations are cited as: Reg (EEC) 2349/84

After the abbreviation of the Regulation comes the name of the Community from which it derives, bracketed: here it is the European Economic Community. There follows the number of the Regulation in the year, here 2349. Finally comes the year, 1984.

Decisions and Directives

Confusingly for the uninitiated, Decisions and Directives are cited quite differently: Dir 89/592/EEC

Here, after the abbreviation, Dir, comes the year of issue, 1989, followed by the number of the Directive in the year, 592. The relevant Community comes at the end, unbracketed.

6.3.3 Source

The texts of all secondary legislation can be found in the Official Journal of the European Communities (the 'OJ' or, in French, 'JO'). Appearing as it does almost every day, the OJ provides regularity of service for the Euro-insomniac, but is generally regarded as an irksome document for the researcher to grapple with, particularly because of some deficiencies in its index.

The OJ is published in two main series:

(1) the 'L' series 'Legislation'; and
(2) the 'C' series 'Communications and Information'.

The 'L' series contains all EC legislation and is itself subdivided into two parts. First, there are the Acts whose publication is obligatory under the treaties, ie Regulations and ECSC Decisions. Secondly, there are those whose publication is not obligatory, ie all other legislation. Indications of particularly important legislation are given by the use of bold type and, on the contents page, by asterisks.

The 'C' series is used to disseminate a variety of categories of information, and a quick look through on a daily basis will keep the researcher in touch with the following: draft legislation; European Parliament opinions on draft legislation; decisions of the European Court of Justice (ECJ) (but not the texts of the judgments), and recent requests for rulings in the ECJ.

Citations to the OJ are relatively straightforward giving the year, series, issue number and page. Thus, 'OJ 1988 L50/18' is the 'L' series OJ, issue number 50, page 18. In some law reports this would appear as '[1988] OJ L50/18'. Sometimes, the precise date of the OJ in question will also be cited.

6.3.4 Tracing secondary legislation

Encyclopedia of European Community Law

The volumes marked 'C' (Numbers I to X) of *Encyclopedia of European Community Law* (Sweet & Maxwell) contain a wide selection of the most important secondary legislation. The volumes are subdivided into Parts referred to by the letter 'C' followed by an arabic number. Thus, for example, C17 is the Part concerned with environmental legislation: this Part can be found in Volume X of the 'C' volumes.

Tracing secondary legislation with a citation

Assuming a citation is to hand, the simplest approach to tracing secondary legislation is to turn to the checklist in Part C18 of Volume X. This lists all the secondary legislation held in the *Encyclopedia*. The list begins with the Regulations, in chronological order: it continues with the Decisions, Directives, Recommendations and Opinions, all intermingled but again in chronological order. The citation is on the left-hand side of the page, and the reference on the right.

Example

Assume that you have a citation for Directive 89/48 of 1989 (the Mutual Recognition of Higher Education Diplomas Directive). This Directive can be traced in the second half of the checklist, remembering that it is Directive Number 48 of 1989: the text is in Part C12 (which happens to be in Volume VI) at paragraph 885.

Tracing secondary legislation without a citation

There are two possible approaches to the problem of tracing secondary legislation without a citation: either to use the index in Volume X, or, alternatively, to second-guess the subject matter, go directly to the relevant Part and scan through the list of Acts at the beginning of that Part.

The starting point will usually be the index, but this is not always as useful as it might be. Thus, only by searching 'Diplomas' or 'Education' would you find the Directive 89/48: neither 'Recognition' nor 'Mutual Recognition' would have thrown up the reference: given that the Directive is entitled 'the Mutual Recognition of Higher Education Diplomas', you might have expected those words to have triggered some reaction.

Consequently, a quick look through the list of legislation at the beginning of Part C12, the 'Right of Establishment' section, might have traced the Directive more quickly.

6.3.5 Checking the status of secondary legislation

'Current Status'

EC legislation may be amended or repealed, and therefore an up-to-date guide to the current status of such legislation is an invaluable aid to the researcher. *European Communities Legislation: Current Status* performs this function. It is published annually in two hardback volumes which are backed up by supplements appearing each May, August and November: each supplement contains an updated index to the complete work.

The hardback volumes are split chronologically, the first covering the period 1952–1980, and the second 1981– date. Each volume is subdivided into years and, within each year, the Regulations and ECSC Decisions are listed first (in the manner of the OJ), followed by the remainder of the secondary legislation. Having traced the legislation, it is possible to see straightaway: whether it is still in force or spent; what amendments and repeals have been made to it; and a brief description of its content.

If no citation is available for the legislation in question, it can be traced using the index of the latest supplement. The entries to the index of this work are based on Community phraseology used in titles to the acts as well as terms in common usage. Thus, to trace the Mutual Recognition of Diplomas Directive, a search under 'Diplomas' will lead to 'Right of establishment and freedom to provide services — mutual recognition of diplomas' 89/48 and 89/49. This will, in turn, lead on to the status of those Directives in Volume 2. A further check on recent developments should then be made in the most recent cumulative supplement.

A telephone facility is also available providing the latest available information in this field.

6.3.6 Checking to see if a Directive has been incorporated into UK law

General

Directives are only binding as to the effect to be achieved, and governments of member states are left to implement EC legislation by incorporation into national law. In the case of the UK, this will be achieved by statute or, more commonly, statutory instrument.

When researching a Directive, it is important to know if national legislation has, in fact, been passed to implement it and, if so, what that legislation is.

Butterworths EC Legislation Implementator

A one-volume book entitled *Butterworths EC Legislation Implementator* appears twice yearly. It is divided into two sections: the first lists, in chronological order, all

Directives which have been implemented by UK legislation, with the target date for implementation and a reference to the relevant UK legislation alongside. Thus if, for example, the researcher wishes to know whether Directive 89/48 (as to Mutual Recognition of Diplomas) has been put into effect in UK law, it could be seen immediately that there was a target date of 4 January 1991 for implementation; furthermore, the relevant UK legislation is the Education (Teachers) Regulations 1989, SI 1989/1319 and the EC (Recognition of Professional Qualifications) Regulations 1991, SI 1991/824. You would need to refer to, say, *Halsbury's Statutory Instruments* for the actual texts of those instruments.

The second section of the book reproduces the latest table from the Annual Report to the European Parliament, listing the Member States which have implemented particular Directives. Considerable care is needed here since the table will usually be out of date.

Encyclopedia of European Community Law

As an alternative to the *Implementator*, a search of the table of selected Community Secondary Legislation at the beginning of Volume A1 ('United Kingdom Sources') of the *Encyclopedia of European Community Law* (Sweet & Maxwell) will provide a reference to the relevant UK legislation as it appears in the 'A' Volume. An advantage of using the *Encyclopedia* is that the text of the statute or statutory instrument can then be examined within the *Encyclopedia* itself. The *Encyclopedia* does not, however, cover all Directives.

6.3.7 Other sources for keeping up to date with secondary legislation

European Current Law is a monthly journal published towards the end of every month with a cumulative index in each supplement. It contains short details of the most important EC legislation, as well as important legislation recently enacted nationally within European (EC and non-EC) countries. The supplements are bound together annually into a hardback volume.

Current Law and *Halsbury's Laws*, which are discussed in **5.2**, contain references to the most important EC legislation.

6.4 INFORMATION ON PROPOSED LEGISLATION

6.4.1 Tracing draft legislation

Brief mention was made in **6.1** of the importance of keeping abreast of proposed legislation. As a result of this demand there are several specialised services which provide regular up-to-date information on European matters for their subscribers. The researcher who does not have the benefit of such a subscription may have to be satisfied with the following sources.

6.4.2 *European Access*

European Access is a bi-monthly bulletin which covers a selection of draft Commission proposals which have not yet been published in the OJ. Such proposals are known as COM documents and are cited accordingly with number and year, followed by the word 'FINAL', which indicates that the draft is a final draft. Generally, earlier drafts will not be within the public domain.

6.4.3 The Official Journal

Draft legislation will appear in the OJ when the Commission seeks an opinion from the European Parliament and the Economic and Social Committee. Further amended drafts may follow. The problem, as ever, with the OJ is the lack of an adequate index for tracing this material.

6.4.4 Other sources

Up-to-date information can often be obtained from the London offices of the European Commission (tel 071-973 1992) and the European Parliament (tel 071-222 0411). The Commission operates an open-door policy so that a telephone call to the official dealing with proposed legislation may save hours of painstaking research. Furthermore, for those on its mailing list, the Commission also publishes free weekly bulletins of the week's developments as well as booklets setting out Commission policy in areas such as competition, environmental and consumer law.

The Financial Times has an excellent European service, and topical information can be obtained from that newspaper.

6.5 CASE-LAW

6.5.1 The courts

Proceedings before the European Courts will be contained in:

(1) the Court of Justice of the European Communities (the 'ECJ'); or
(2) the Court of First Instance of the European Communities, established by the Single European Act of 1986.

Additionally, there will be many cases heard in the national courts of the Member States which are of importance to the EC law researcher.

6.5.2 Citation of EC cases

Cases in the ECJ

ECJ cases are cited with their names and additionally their numbers. A case may thus be cited as *British Aerospace and Others v EC Commission* C292/90. The letter 'C' (short for 'Cour') indicates this to be an ECJ case: furthermore, it is the Case number 292 of 1990. It is important to remember that the year in the citation refers to the year when the case was filed, rather than the year of the decision. This can cause endless confusion.

Cases in the Court of First Instance

First instance cases are cited in the same way as those in the ECJ except that the number is prefixed by the letter 'T' (short for 'Tribunal') instead of 'C'.

6.5.3 The law reports

The ECR

The Official Law Reports are called Reports of Cases before the Court (ECR). Since the reports have to be translated from French into all the official languages of the EC, it is usual to have to wait two years or so before a report appears in the ECR. Needless to say, researchers look for other means of obtaining essential information from the cases, and one can usually acquire copies of the judgments and opinions of the Advocate-General from the Court Registry. There is a subscription service for such material. Hardy souls who can deal with the reports in French have an advantage since they will often appear in that language first.

Common Market Law Reports (CMLR)

The Common Market Law Reports are an unofficial series of reports which appear monthly and contain a selection of ECJ and first-instance decisions, together with certain Commission Decisions and reports of cases before the courts of member states which have a bearing on EC law. These reports are bound at the end of the year and cited as follows: [1981] 2 CMLR 362.

This refers to Volume 2 of the CMLR of 1981 at page 362.

There is now also a separate Anti-Trust Supplement to the CMLR dealing only with Competition cases; these are hived off into separate volumes, but are cited in the same way as other reports.

The Official Journal

The 'C' series of the *Official Journal* will give indications of orders and judgments made in the courts, but nothing more. Indication that judgment has been given, however, will tell the researcher that the Court Registry should have the judgment available within one month or so.

Other sources

A number of important decisions are reported in the law reports contained in newspapers. *Current Law* and *Halsbury's Laws* also provide summaries of the most important cases on a monthly basis.

Chapter 7

LEXIS

7.1 INTRODUCTION

7.1.1 Electronic libraries

Not all law libraries consist of printed material, for these are increasingly being supplemented by electronic libraries where the material is held on a computer as a database. This is accessible to the researcher via a special terminal or a personal computer equipped with the appropriate software. In some cases, the database is available in the office in a physical form, for example as a set of compact disks. In other cases, the size and complexity of the database is such that it must be held centrally; the researcher's terminal or personal computer is then connected to the central computer through the telephone system.

7.1.2 Training

LEXIS is the largest and best-known example of a remote database for lawyers. The researcher requires a full training course, with much practical experience and supervision, before he can be a confident and competent user, although he does not have to be a good typist – one finger will suffice! The purpose of this chapter is to provide only a brief introduction to what LEXIS is and what it does.

7.1.3 LEXIS

Since LEXIS is an American system (the database is located in Ohio), most of its materials relate to the law of the USA, but materials relevant to the UK and the European Community are also held on it, as well as other foreign material. Butterworth Telepublishing Ltd makes the service available here and is responsible for the British material.

7.1.4 Primary sources

LEXIS is essentially a vast electronic store of words, ie the complete text of legal materials. Most are primary sources of law (case reports, statutes and statutory instruments) although much secondary material (such as the text of legal journals) is also available.

7.1.5 Advantages

There are a number of advantages in using legal materials in this format.

(1) The sheer quantity of materials available, at the touch of a button, greatly exceeds what any one paper library could provide.
(2) The material is more up to date, as additional cases, statutes, etc can be added (and existing material can be amended) centrally; thus, the latest version is instantly available to users worldwide.
(3) Relevant items can be located very rapidly (usually in a few seconds), even by a researcher who starts with limited information (such as a half-remembered case name or phrase from a judgment or statute) which would be an inadequate basis for more traditional methods of research.

7.1.6 Hardware

The researcher has either a 'dedicated terminal', ie a computer specially designed for accessing LEXIS and capable of doing nothing else, or a personal computer or terminal which the researcher uses for other purposes but which also has special software for accessing LEXIS. In either case, the machine is linked by telephone to Butterworth Telepublishing Ltd in London and from there to the computer in Ohio. The user's machine has a screen, a keyboard and a printer which can print whatever appears on screen.

7.1.7 Points to remember

The researcher needs to remember a few very basic points if he is to make sensible use of this incredibly powerful tool.

(1) LEXIS is an information retrieval system, not a problem-solving 'expert system'. It finds materials and leaves the researcher to understand and apply them.

(2) LEXIS is literal. It finds words but does not understand them. When asked to find references to a bank it will include banks of rivers as well as banks which deal in money.

(3) LEXIS is interactive. The researcher is conducting a dialogue with the database. When he sees the result of his first search, he may narrow, widen or change the direction of his search. He may do this several times before finding everything he wants. Therefore, LEXIS is best used by the researcher in person, rather than by someone who is delegated with the task.

(4) LEXIS is full text. What it contains is not a summary and all but the most common words (the, an, etc) can be searched for.

(5) LEXIS is expensive, being charged for primarily on the basis of the number and duration of searches made. Effective use saves the researcher time and produces better results than relying on paper libraries alone, so the expense is then justified. Ineffective use can be wasteful.

7.2 CONTENTS OF LEXIS

7.2.1 Libraries and files

The database is divided into 'libraries' which are subdivided into 'files'. A search can only be made in one file at a time, although the system makes it easy to repeat a search in another file in the same or another library.

7.2.2 Primary sources

The primary English materials are contained in the English General library (enggen) the main files of which are as follows:

(1) the cases file (cases) contains the store of cases drawn from general and specialist law reports, plus an enormous number of transcripts of unreported cases;

(2) the statutes file (stat) contains all public general Acts in their up-to-date form, ie as amended by later legislation, with annotations showing the source of amendments and their date of commencement;

(3) the statutory instrument file (si) similarly contains the full texts of current statutory instruments in updated form;

(4) the combined file (statis) allows a single search to be made in both stat and si files.

7.2.3 Journals

Another useful library is the United Kingdom Journals library (ukjnl), which contains such materials as the *Law Society Gazette*.

7.2.4 European Community etc

The case-law of the European Court and European Court of Human Rights is found in the European Communities library (eurcom) cases file. The European Community has its own legal database (CELEX) consisting of Community legislation and this is made available to LEXIS users as the European Community file (eclaw) of the International library (intlaw).

7.2.5 Foreign materials

An English lawyer may also need to consult Australian, New Zealand, Irish, Scottish, US and other materials. The French libraries are in French and their user must be prepared to use French LEXIS terminology.

7.2.6 Documents and segments

Each file is made up of documents. A case, section of a statute, journal article, etc constitutes a document. Each document is, in turn, divided into segments containing, for example: name of case; date of decision; name of court; names of judges, etc.

7.3 MAKING A SEARCH

7.3.1 Some typical examples

The researcher will type the search using the keyboard. The search may consist of one word, for example, he could search for every occurrence in English cases of the name 'Caldwell'. He is more likely to want to search for a number of words, some being alternatives and others being within a certain proximity of each other in the text. The following may serve as examples.

(1) In the cases file of enggen: *Caldwell and reckless*. This search would find all cases where both words occur in the same case.
(2) In the same file: *Caldwell w/50 recklessness*. This search would find all cases where these two words occur within 50 words of each other (any number can be specified, not just 50).
(3) In the same file: *criminal damage or arson*. This search would find all cases in which either of these phrases occurs.
(4) In the same file: *recklessness w/40 criminal damage or arson*. This search would find any case where either of the phrases 'criminal damage' or 'arson' occurs within 40 words of the word 'recklessness'.

7.3.2 Connectors and other features

The words 'and', 'or' and 'w/-' are called connectors, the 'w/-' being the proximity connector; they are vital in composing sensible searches. There are a number of other features of the LEXIS language which make the user's life easier.

(1) A search for a word will also find a regular plural or possessive form; thus girl will find girls, girl's and girls' but child will not find children.
(2) A search for wom*n will find woman and women.
(3) A search for negligen! will find negligent, negligently and negligence.

(4) LEXIS does not distinguish between upper and lower case letters in a search, so a search for 'woman' will find 'Woman'.

7.3.3 Using the segments

The segments into which a document is divided allow the researcher who is familiar with their names and contents to make sophisticated and precise searches. Broadly, the search should include the name of the segment with, in brackets, the words which the user wishes to find in that segment. Some examples may help.

(1) In the cases file of enggen: *name (caldwell) and reckles! and court (lords or privy) and date aft (1970)*. This search would find any case where the word 'Caldwell' forms part of the name; the word 'reckless', 'recklessly' or 'recklessness' appears in the text; the court is the House of Lords or the Judicial Committee of the Privy Council; and, the case was decided after 1970.

(2) In the stat file of enggen: *title (personal injuries and 1948) and section (2)*. This search would find the Law Reform (Personal Injuries) Act 1948, s2, as amended by subsequent legislation.

(3) In the si file of enggen: *authority (financial services and 1986)*. This search would find all statutory instruments made under the Financial Services Act 1986.

(4) In the same file: *title (1988 and 1058)*. This search would find the statutory instrument corresponding with this reference number.

(5) In the *Law Society Gazette* file (lsg) of the ukjnl library: *author (margaret rutherford) and dragon*. This search would find two articles by this writer in which reference is made to a dragon.

7.4 USING THE MATERIAL RETRIEVED

7.4.1 Viewing material

If LEXIS produces a number of documents in response to a search, it is easy to call up on screen a list of the documents with their references. This list is called the 'cites'. Any of the documents can be called up in full on screen. The researcher may prefer to go straight to the passage in which his search terms appear. The facility to do this is known as 'kwic' (key word in context). It is easy to move about the retrieved material, ie from document to document and from page to page and back again.

7.4.2 Printing

Anything which appears on the screen can be printed out for further reference and study. A useful technique is to print out the cites and look them up in a paper library, returning to LEXIS for documents which prove to be unavailable in that library.

7.5 LEXIS IS USER FRIENDLY

The researcher cannot break LEXIS by keying the wrong entry or pressing the wrong button. The computer itself will help to correct errors by offering advice and instructions on the screen. The researcher also has access, by telephone, to the customer service department of Butterworth Telepublishing Ltd.

Chapter 8

THE RESULTS OF LEGAL RESEARCH

8.1 RECORDING AND REPORTING

Once the legal research is complete, is it any use? Good legal research will provide an answer to a problem. If it does not, then it has probably not been done properly.

It is important to remember what the problem is and therefore why the research is being done. This will lead the researcher through the maze of source materials to find the answers he needs to solve the client's problem.

As was stated at **2.2.4**, the last stage of the research process is its application to the client's problem.

If the legal research has been performed by someone other than the client's adviser, it is necessary that the results of that research be clearly communicated. Even if the adviser has himself performed research, it is as well to make a clear record of the legal basis for advice. Clearly, the nature of the record will vary with the research – in particular whether the researcher knows the full background to the client's problem – but the following points should be borne in mind:

(1) the report should be a summary of the research notes;
(2) it should give references for the sources which proved useful, as well as the result of the research, so that the research can be checked;
(3) it should state the date when the research was completed, and the dates of the sources used;
(4) the results can be presented in note form, using technical language if appropriate, and assuming knowledge of the legal background;
(5) if the factual context is known, the results should be applied to the facts, and brief notes made of obvious practical implications.

PART III

ORAL COMMUNICATION SKILLS

Chapter 9

INTRODUCTION TO ORAL COMMUNICATION SKILLS

Chapter 9 contents
General
Listening
Questioning
Non-verbal communication

9.1 GENERAL

> One-third of what is said is not heard
> One-third is heard but not understood
> One-third is understood – but may not be accepted
> (adapted from a passage in *The Skills of Negotiating* by Bill Scott)

All solicitors need to possess good oral communication skills in order to defeat the 'one-third rule' (above) and to become effective interviewers (Chapter 10), negotiators (Chapter 11) or advocates (Chapter 12).

Solicitors also need to establish and maintain good working relationships with their colleagues in the office (whether professional or administrative), with members of other professions whom they have to consult or instruct, and with representatives of official bodies (eg court staff).

Although oral communication skills are largely based on common sense, people's ability to use them varies enormously. Some people are naturally better than others, but everyone is capable of improvement. Like any other skill (driving a car, playing a musical instrument, playing a sport), performance can be improved by learning specific skills and techniques, and then practising them.

At first, practising new techniques can feel artificial ('It's just not me') but after a while the technique usually becomes second nature (like changing gear in a car). However, skills training should not be allowed to suppress natural ability, and it is possible to be a competent interviewer, negotiator or advocate without necessarily having to perform every technique by the book. It is a question of balance; but success comes through practising sound techniques. Brilliant mavericks are rare.

This chapter introduces those aspects of oral communication skills which are common to interviewing, negotiation and advocacy. Chapters 10–12 explain how the skills apply to each of these activities.

9.2 LISTENING

In order to advise a client, or to persuade an opponent or the court, solicitors have first to *demonstrate* that they have both heard and understood what the other has said.

This involves listening carefully to what is being said. However, listening is an underrated skill which requires considerable concentration. Listening as a solicitor is very different from listening in the context of ordinary social discourse, where interchanges are shorter and more fluid and where there is less need to pick up every nuance or recall precisely what was said. Listening as a solicitor is also different from listening to lectures, where students do not necessarily have to interrelate with the lecturer and may be able to copy up notes from elsewhere later. Nevertheless, students who are good listeners in lectures will find that this skill will help them enormously in practice.

Most authorities on oral communication skills make a distinction between 'passive listening' and 'active listening'.

9.2.1 Passive listening

Passive listening involves using silences and other unobtrusive signals to encourage the speaker to continue. For example, when interviewing, negotiating or conducting advocacy, the solicitor might want to induce the speaker to carry on speaking and thereby perhaps volunteer a crucial piece of information.

Silences can be embarrassing in normal social situations, so many people learn during their upbringing to avoid them. Yet silence is one of the most powerful techniques available to a solicitor. It may require a conscious effort to remain silent for longer than normal in the hope that the speaker will fill the void with more information.

Other non-obtrusive signals a solicitor may give the speaker to encourage him to continue include:

- eye contact
- posture
- nodding
- acknowledgments ('Uh, huh')
- express invitations ('Go on')

9.2.2 Active listening

Active listening, as the phrase suggests, involves more obtrusive techniques which demonstrate to the other person that the solicitor has both heard and understood.

The most common form of active listening is summarising, ie giving a short, clear precis of what the speaker has just said. Like silence, the technique is not regularly employed in social conversations and so requires a conscious effort.

Summarising is also used by solicitors to check the effectiveness of communication in the reverse direction, ie that the other person has heard and understood the solicitor.

9.3 QUESTIONING

Questioning skills are well-known tools of the solicitor's trade. Questions can be classified according to the breadth of the response they allow, ie as open or closed questions.

9.3.1 Open questions

Open questions give maximum freedom to the person being questioned, they encourage expansion, and they do not seek to influence the content of the reply.

Examples
'So what happened next?'
'What were your reactions to that?'
'How did you respond to the offer?'

'Why did you do that?'
'Tell me about your relationship with the managing director.'

Open questions do not necessarily have to be worded as questions: 'Tell me . . .' is a phrase which can be used to invite an open response.

9.3.2 Closed questions

Closed questions invite a narrow answer, from a few words or a sentence to a 'Yes'/'No' reply (sometimes called 'Yes/No questions').

Examples
'Were you also carrying a knife?'
'Did you accept the offer?'

One particular form of closed question is the leading question. For example, the questioner might deliberately seek to influence the content of the reply by asking a question which encourages a particular answer 'So you must have been drunk, mustn't you?'

9.4 NON-VERBAL COMMUNICATION

Non-verbal communication includes eye contact, posture and gestures and is often called 'body language'.

Careful observation of the body language of other people can provide clues as to how they are feeling, or how they are responding to advice or to an argument, and can therefore be influential in deciding how to proceed. However, tread cautiously, because the clue might not be conclusive: the interpretation of body language is controversial, and is subject to cultural variations. Be aware of non-verbal communication, but do not allow it to distract you from everything else.

Similarly, awareness of how your own body language affects both yourself and others can help in deciding how to convey your message more effectively. Although it is sometimes said that one cannot (or should not) 'fake' body language, cause and effect are often interrelated. Sitting with your arms tightly folded and your legs crossed, or nervously drumming your fingers or tapping your foot, can affect your own feelings as well as influencing others' perceptions of you. Sitting or standing in a physically relaxed manner can help you feel more relaxed.

A useful book is *Body Language* by Alan Pease (Sheldon Press).

Chapter 10

INTERVIEWING AND ADVISING

10.1 OBJECTIVES OF A LEGAL INTERVIEW

An interview between a solicitor and a client has four principal objectives:

(1) to establish good rapport between the solicitor and the client;

(2) to obtain relevant information from the client;

(3) to advise the client;

(4) to help the client reach appropriate decisions.

Other legal interviews (eg with witnesses) usually serve more limited purposes.

This chapter concentrates on the skills required by the solicitor in conducting the first interview with a client.

10.2 COMMON FAILINGS

There are many reasons why a solicitor may fail to achieve the above objectives. Some common examples follow.

10.2.1 Obstacles created by the solicitor

The solicitor might have set up an obstacle to communication by:

- inadequate preparation
- creating the wrong physical environment
- failing to listen
- failing to appear to listen
- talking too much
- interrupting too frequently
- making a premature diagnosis
- taking too narrow a view of client needs
- restricting the areas in which the client feels free to talk

10.2.2 Client inhibitions

The client may suffer from an inhibition which the solicitor fails to appreciate or fails to help the client to overcome. For example, the client may:

- fear that full disclosure will damage his self-esteem or be a career-threat
- think that full disclosure will damage the case or the proposed transaction
- expect the solicitor to do all the talking
- find it difficult to talk to a solicitor of a different sex, race, class or age
- assume certain information to be irrelevant to the problem
- have a greater need to talk about a more immediate problem than the one identified by the solicitor

The solicitor should think about these potential obstacles before the interview and try to be aware of their potential impact during it.

The skills referred to later in this chapter will help you to counteract these obstacles.

10.3 TWO MAJOR INGREDIENTS IN EFFECTIVE INTERVIEWING

10.3.1 Interpersonal and communication skills

In an interview the relevant interpersonal and communication skills are those needed to:

(1) establish and maintain good rapport with the client;
(2) obtain a full account of all the issues concerning the client;
(3) give effective advice;
(4) help the client to reach appropriate decisions.

10.3.2 Structure and management

Structure and management involve:

(1) creating an appropriate environment for the interview;
(2) preparing for the interview;
(3) using an efficient 'model' to structure the interview;
(4) taking adequate notes;
(5) discussing costs;
(6) explaining the appropriate follow-up.

A well-managed interview will help to promote good rapport with the client. Moreover, a client who likes and has confidence in the solicitor will usually forgive (or even fail to notice) any technical shortcomings in the conduct of the interview.

10.4 THE INTERPERSONAL AND COMMUNICATION SKILLS

10.4.1 Listening – an undervalued skill

Encouraging a client to tell his/her own story is generally a more effective way of gathering information than attempting to elicit the story by a series of closed questions. Listening skills are therefore paramount until you have a reasonably full version of the case.

Where the client is verbose, prone to irrelevancy or where there is little time, a more forceful (braking) role may be required, but this should only be adopted when absolutely necessary.

Listening is an undervalued and frequently under-used skill which involves a range of techniques to sustain information-giving.

Silence

In every day social conversation, periods of silence can sometimes cause embarrassment and create a need in others to fill the gap.

However, in an interview, periods of silence give the client time to collect thoughts, to tell the story as he sees and remembers it, and to deal with the feelings it creates. You must therefore learn to control the natural urge to fill silences.

Body language
You should give conscious thought to how body language may help or hinder building good rapport with the client. For example:

(1) eye contact: a friendly, but not a prolonged stare;
(2) posture: leaning slightly towards the client;
(3) head-nodding: but not too much;
(4) avoiding irritating/distracting mannerisms, eg pen-tapping, foot-drumming, etc.

Acknowledgments
Brief indications (without interrupting) showing attention, interest, and understanding, such as:

'Yes, I see'

'. . . in Brussels?'

'Mhmmmm'.

Invitations to continue/elaborate
Examples are:

'Go on'

'What happened?'

'Tell me more about that'.

Summarising
Restating the facts which the client has outlined, either in the form of a paraphrase or longer summary, for example:

'You mean that . . .'

'If I understand you correctly, what you are saying is . . .'

This technique provides a test of your understanding of what has been said, and actively demonstrates to the client that you have genuinely been listening. However, excessive use of the summarising technique (or merely 'parroting' the client's words) can be counter-productive. The client may think you are slow, dim-witted or insensitive to his desire to get on with the interview.

Reflecting feeling
This involves letting the client know that you have understood and accepted the client's feelings. It is therefore useful in building rapport, for example: 'I can quite see why you feel so angry about this'.

The technique involves expressing empathy with the client's feelings, not being judgmental about them.

Awareness of the client's feelings is gained from observing and correctly interpreting the client's body language, not merely from listening to the client's words and tone of voice.

The ability to reflect feeling is particularly important where the client's emotions will be a major factor in the handling of a case, for example in matrimonial cases.

However, reflecting feeling may also be appropriate in interviews which may appear to be less personal, for example when a commercial client has anxieties about losing self-esteem within the company if a transaction fails to reach a satisfactory conclusion.

10.4.2 Questioning

In an initial interview, a solicitor needs to gather information on:

(1) the nature of the client's problem or proposed transaction;
(2) the relevant background facts;
(3) the client's feelings and objectives.

Whilst most of this information may be obtained through use of the listening techniques discussed above, it will usually be necessary to clarify and probe further by questioning.

For an initial interview, particularly in the early stages, open questions usually have more advantages than closed questions and failure to recognise this leads many interviews into an interviewer-dominated style.

10.4.3 Open questions

The advantages of open questions are that they:

- allow the client to select the subject matter
- allow the client to select the information the client believes to be relevant
- allow the client to start with information about which the client feels comfortable
- enable the client to get things 'off his chest'
- give the client freedom to reflect and to feel more actively involved in the interview
- encourage memory by association, which may produce information which would be overlooked if the client were asked only closed questions

The disadvantages are that they:

- may initially produce insufficient information
- may encourage the client to verbosity and/or irrelevance
- may inhibit a reticent client

10.4.4 Closed questions

The advantages of closed questions are that they:

- are a good method of obtaining precise details
- may guide a client less stressfully through a sensitive area
- may give confidence to an initially reticent or anxious client
- may help to prompt memory
- help to clarify and probe areas of ambiguity or uncertainty
- may quieten a verbose client

The disadvantages are that they:

- may lead to an over-clinical or 'processing' style of interview
- may deprive the client of the opportunity to state the case in his own words
- may inhibit rapport
- reduce the opportunity to listen to and observe the client, and to understand his needs
- may lead the solicitor to miss important areas of information because the client is not allowed to associate ideas freely

- may even result in the solicitor's directing the interview down a totally irrelevant path

10.4.5 The 'T-funnel'

The use of open questions followed by closed questions is sometimes known as the T-funnel sequence of questioning:

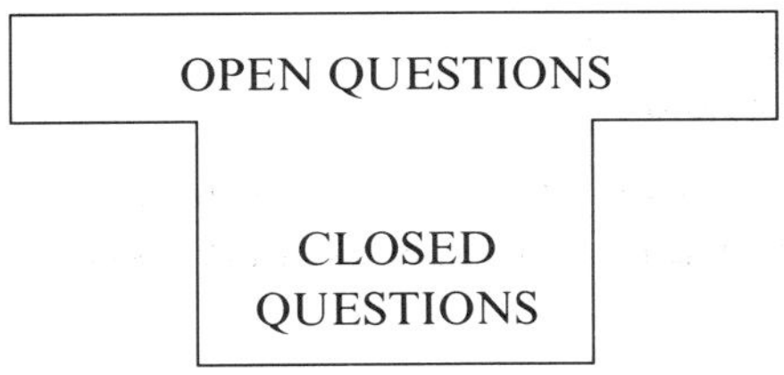

The solicitor focuses on a topic with a series of open questions. Only after the open questions cease to be productive should they be narrowed into closed questions.

Premature use of closed questions may distort the response or lead to important details being omitted.

10.4.6 Further clarification and probing

In the middle and final stages of an interview, it will often be necessary to probe further:

- to resolve remaining areas of ambiguity
- to jog the client's memory
- to clarify client needs and reaction to consequences of action
- to discover how the client will respond to the legal process (in litigation) or to a counter-argument or proposal (negotiating a transaction)

The following are some techniques which may be used to achieve these objectives:

Going back one stage

This involves taking the client back one stage in the narrative and inviting the client to relive the sequence of events in order to jog the memory:

> 'Take me through that again but starting from *before* you were approaching the road junction.'

There is a danger that the client may fill any gaps in the narrative by supplying facts which are incorrect but which the client (often quite sincerely) believes must inevitably have occurred.

Leading questions

Leading questions are sometimes used (appropriately) to help clients to convey something which they may have difficulty in articulating in their own words:

> 'So you've had disagreements with the managing director before?'

> 'So sexual intercourse did take place on that occasion?'

Prefacing a question with explanation

This can counteract the client perceiving your question as irrelevant or allay the client's anxiety in a sensitive area. For example:

> 'I know you're very confident of being acquitted but, if you *are* convicted, the

> magistrates will sentence you immediately. For that reason I now need to ask you some questions about your financial circumstances.'

There is, however, a danger that the explanation may influence (and therefore distort) the client's reply.

Cross-checking
Cross-checking tests the consistency of the facts in order to reveal any gaps or contradictions.

Devil's advocate
To play devil's advocate is to suggest to the client a different and adverse interpretation of his story. For example:

> 'If you're so sure that the accident wasn't your fault, why did you say to the other motorist: "I'm sorry – I just didn't see you coming"?'

It is generally advisable to warn the client in advance that you intend to play devil's advocate and to give reasons for so doing; otherwise, your apparent hostility is likely to damage rapport.

Checklists
Some interviews lend themselves to the use of checklists.

Used appropriately, a checklist has the obvious advantage that essential information is unlikely to be overlooked. A checklist also provides you with a concise and convenient source of information for speedy future reference.

However, interviewing a client simply by running through a checklist, particularly at the beginning of the interview, may inhibit effective communication. The client may well feel that you are merely 'processing a case' rather than listening to the client's unique personal problem.

Indeed, premature use of a checklist (ie before a correct diagnosis of the problem has been made) can waste valuable time while a mass of irrelevant information is accumulated.

10.5 STRUCTURE AND MANAGEMENT

10.5.1 Before the interview

The environment
It is important that the interview should take place in an environment which will help rather than hinder effective communication. The aim should be to create an atmosphere in which the client will feel calm and relaxed and which will give a favourable impression of you and your firm.

You should therefore ensure:

(1) that the client will be physically comfortable;
(2) that the interview will be free from unnecessary interruptions;
(3) that the office surroundings convey a sense of well-organised professionalism without being austere and/or impersonal.

Consider the different impressions which the following could have on the client's perception of you and your firm:

Appearance	*Possible interpretation*
Bare walls, bare chairs, bare table	Austere and impersonal?
Desk heaped with files and letters in no apparent order	Disorganised and chaotic?
Potted plants, soft lights, carpets and curtains, a Modigliani, sofas, executive 'toys'	'Does he do any work here?' and 'How much is all this going to cost me?'

Seating arrangements may also help or hinder effective communication. Views on this topic differ and an arrangement which seems friendly and welcoming to one client may strike another as over-familiar or even invasive.

However, as far as possible, the arrangement should be one in which:

(1) the solicitor and client can clearly see and hear each other;
(2) the client does not feel kept at a distance at one extreme or invaded at the other;
(3) the solicitor and (if necessary) the client can make written notes in comfort.

The traditional arrangement in which the solicitor and client face each other from opposite sides of the solicitor's desk will usually satisfy the above criteria, provided the desk is not piled high with files and papers. It is also the arrangement which most clients will be expecting.

However, depending on the personality of the client and the nature of the matter, you may judge that a less formal arrangement, perhaps without the intervening desk, would be more relaxing for the client and therefore more conducive to communication.

Furthermore, there may be other specific occasions (eg where the client needs to explain a plan, diagram or map to the solicitor) when sitting alongside the client is the only effective arrangement.

You should therefore consider the possibility of other arrangements and be able and willing to adopt them whenever appropriate.

The above comments presuppose that the interview will take place in an environment over which you have some degree of control, most commonly in your own office or in an interview room within the firm's offices. However, you should appreciate that even a first interview may, for a variety of reasons, take place in surroundings (eg hospital ward, prison cell, crowded court corridor, etc) over which you will have little or no control.

Preparing for the interview

Where possible/appropriate, you should:

(1) obtain background information on the client (and the client's business);
(2) request relevant documents and consider them in advance;
(3) refresh your memory on an area of law, being careful not to pre-judge the issues or 'pigeon-hole' the client;
(4) make a checklist;
(5) ensure that the interview will be free from interruptions (especially the telephone).

10.5.2 The model

What is a model?

A model is merely a predetermined structure to be adopted by the solicitor during a client interview.

It divides the interview into a logically ordered sequence of distinct stages, each of which serves a distinct function and requires the use of different interviewing skills.

Example

GREETING

---

(1) PRELIMINARIES
(2) OBTAINING THE FACTS
(3) FILLING IN THE DETAIL
(4) ADVISING
(5) CLOSING

PARTING

The model is based on sound principles and will aid the acquisition of interviewing skills. It has been designed to be simple to understand and implement. Students are therefore advised to follow the stages in the model.

What now follows is a step-by-step account of each successive stage in the model, indicating the purpose of each stage and which skills need to be employed.

10.5.3 Greeting

Judgments of other people's character and abilities are often made within a few minutes of a meeting. (The popular phrase is 'You never get a second chance to make a first impression'.)

You should therefore give full attention to the client in the first minutes of the interview and do everything possible to create a relaxed and friendly relationship.

Thus you should:

(1) ensure that the client is not left to find his or her own way to your room through a bewildering maze of corridors;
(2) make contact immediately by handshake, eye contact, verbal greeting and use of the client's name.

The above points may seem obvious, but they are extremely important.

After greeting, it is a matter of judgment how quickly you proceed to the business at hand, but most clients will have been rehearsing what they wish to say and will be ready to begin at once.

Consider the impact on the client of the following choice of words and expressions:

'So, where shall we start?'

'What's the problem, then?'

'Thank you for sending me the documentation . . . It seems to me . . .'

'Things don't look too good, do they?'

'Don't worry, we'll sort this out for you.'

'Funny, this is the sixth one we've had in like this in the last month.'

'My secretary tells me it's a personal injury case. What exactly happened?'

'You rang earlier. It's about the marriage I gather?'

'Excuse the mess. Just give me a minute while I try to find a note-pad.'

'This is the one, I think. Now then, where are we? . . . Let me see . . . dah dah dah dah . . . Oh yes that's right, a spot of the old GBH isn't it?'

10.5.4 Preliminaries

Objective

The objective of this stage of the interview is to ascertain the general nature of the client's problem and reason for seeking legal advice (a client overview). For example: 'I want to set up in business/make a will/get a divorce/buy a house/claim damages after a car accident'.

The above are straightforward examples, but it is not always possible for the client neatly to 'pigeon-hole' the matter in a way which is helpful to a lawyer.

Furthermore, some clients find it difficult to think through and/or articulate precisely what their desires and needs are. For example:

'Well, it is rather a long and involved story but three years ago I met this bloke called Douglas . . .'

In such a situation it is almost always better to let the client give an unhindered account of the matter rather than to interrupt and try to force the client to classify it. Thus the preliminaries stage will merge into the next stage ('Obtaining the facts').

Even if the client can give a brief description of the matter, it is vital that you should avoid making a premature diagnosis. For example, a woman who says, 'I want a divorce' may say so in the mistaken belief that taking divorce proceedings is necessary in order to resolve her more immediate problems, such as obtaining financial support, protection from violence, etc.

Nevertheless, obtaining a client overview has two advantages, as it enables you to set a timetable for the rest of the interview and to discuss costs.

Timetable

Because the client or solicitor may be under time constraints, such as having a car on a parking meter, children to collect or an appointment at court, it is helpful for most clients if you can give an estimate at this stage of the probable length of the interview and say whether a second interview is likely to be necessary.

Costs

Clients naturally tend to be concerned about the cost of the interview. It can therefore be reassuring to tackle this at an early stage.

In this connection, obtaining a client overview can help you to decide:

(1) whether the matter and the client are covered by some form of legal aid; or
(2) how much the client is likely to be charged.

For more on costs see **10.6** and the LPC Resource Book *Pervasive Topics* (Jordans, 1993), Part II Professional Conduct.

The skills

The skills are:

(1) Listening;
(2) Open questions;
(3) No (or very brief) note-taking; and
(4) No premature diagnosis.

10.5.5 Obtaining the facts

Objective

The objective is to obtain the client's account of the facts or of the proposed transaction.

The skills

The objective should be achieved by encouraging the client to give an account of the matter in his or her own words with as little interruption from you as possible.

You should concentrate on using the various listening techniques discussed in **10.4.1** and confine questions to open questions which will encourage the client to continue the narrative.

There will be ample opportunity in the next stage of the interview ('Filling in the detail') to clarify matters. You should therefore resist any temptation to do so at this stage, because a series of closed questions can easily destroy the client's concentration.

For the same reason, making written notes should, if possible, be restricted to what can be written without interrupting the client's narrative flow.

This comparatively passive role can be a difficult one to master. It does, however, enable you to maintain eye contact with the client and to observe the client's general demeanour and manner of delivery. This is very helpful in building rapport with the client and in picking up body language signals about the client's feelings.

Skills summary

(1) Listening.
(2) Questioning – mainly open questions.
(3) Brief note-taking.

10.5.6 Filling in the detail

Objective

The objective is to ensure that you obtain a full and accurate understanding and record of the relevant facts and of the client's wishes and objectives.

The skills

You will not usually be able to give the client effective advice immediately after the client has completed his or her account of the matter in the 'Obtaining the facts' stage.

In most cases it will be necessary to ask the client to fill gaps or explain discrepancies in the narrative or to supply information which the client had not considered to be relevant.

You will also need to take more comprehensive written notes and generally to check that you have correctly understood what the client has said. It may also be necessary to examine documents.

This is the stage of the interview during which the solicitor assumes a more active and directive role.

Questioning skills become more important although, even when asking the client to focus on one particular aspect of the matter, it is generally best to use the T-funnel approach (discussed in **10.4.5**), in other words to see what information can be elicited in response to open questions before pinning down the client with more specific closed questions.

This is the stage in the interview when it may be necessary to use some of the clarifying and probing techniques (see **10.4.6**) to jog the client's memory or to explore apparent discrepancies or weaknesses in the client's version of events.

During this stage, it will often be helpful to summarise what the client has said in order to double check that you have correctly understood what he has told you.

Skills summary

(1) Questioning – the T-funnel approach
(2) Note-taking
(3) Summarising
(4) Clarifying and probing
(5) Examining documents.

10.5.7 Advising

Objectives

The solicitor:

(1) explains the legal position of the client;
(2) discusses with the client the main options (both legal and non-legal);
(3) helps the client to reach a decision/give instructions.

Explaining the client's legal position

The client's legal position should be explained in a manner which is simple and comprehensible. You should therefore avoid jargon. Furthermore, you should be aware that the amount of information which a client can absorb is limited.

This is the first interview. Therefore, if:

(1) the matter is not routine;
(2) you do not have experience in the particular area of law;
(3) the client does not insist on preliminary 'off the cuff' advice; or
(4) the matter is not urgent,

it is quite proper to adjourn the interview at this stage to give yourself an opportunity to carry out research prior to tendering advice.

Clients do not always need or expect to be given immediate advice.

Discussing the main options

The client is generally less interested in being given a detailed resumé of the law than in being told what courses of action are open to him. You should therefore identify all possible options and discuss the relative merits of each option thoroughly with the client.

You should try to involve the client in the discussion so that you can jointly weigh the advantages and disadvantages of each option.

Helping the client to reach a decision

All major decisions concerning the case or transaction are for the client to make. It is the client's case, not the solicitor's. However, opinion is divided on how far the solicitor may recommend a course of action for the client.

There are two schools of thought.

(1) The non-directive school suggests that a solicitor should only present the options and leave it entirely to the client to decide which to follow. The advice is characterised by the preamble, 'On the one hand X but on the other hand Y. However it is for you to decide'.

    This approach may avoid a charge of negligence if the route followed by the client transpires to be the wrong option. However, it is not particularly helpful to the client. Given the status, experience and cost of solicitors, clients often expect a recommendation.

(2) The directive school involves the solicitor in taking greater control of the decision-making process.

A combination of each approach is appropriate in most cases. It is important to explain the realistic options to the client and to explore the positive and negative consequences of each. Provided the client actively participates in this explorative discussion and the solicitor actively seeks the client's views and preferences, the decision will often be clear.

Furthermore, if the decision to be made is non-urgent, difficult or complex, the client should defer taking it and take time to reach a considered opinion.

The skills

It will already be apparent that the most important skill to be employed during this stage is clarity of expression, an important aspect of which is the avoidance of bewildering legal jargon.

You must find a way of explaining the law and the available options in a way which the client can readily understand.

It is important always to bear in mind that advice which is accurate, eloquent and faultlessly reasoned but which is incomprehensible to the client is no advice at all, and that your failure in this regard will almost certainly render the interview a complete waste of the client's time and money.

10.5.8 Closing

Objective

To bring the interview to an appropriate close.

The interview should not close without the solicitor first ensuring that the client:

(1) has been given an opportunity to discuss all matters and concerns;
(2) knows what action will be taken by the solicitor (and when);

(3) knows what action the solicitor expects the client to take (and when);
(4) knows how and when the next solicitor/client contact (if any) will take place;
(5) understands the costs position (if not explained previously).

The skills

(1) Summarising (perhaps in writing).
(2) Asking open question, for example: 'Is there anything else which you want to talk about?'
(3) Using plain words/avoiding jargon for all explanations given to the client.

10.5.9 Parting

When the interview is over, the solicitor should accompany the client back to the reception area.

The parting should be friendly and courteous.

10.5.10 Follow-up

What action, if any, is required after the interview differs from case to case.

However, the solicitor should:

(1) consider confirming advice in writing;
(2) take appropriate action as promptly as possible;
(3) report progress and/or reasons for delay to the client at regular intervals.

10.6 DISCUSSING COSTS

10.6.1 When?

There is no single optimum time during the interview to discuss costs.

The general rule is to tackle the matter as early as practicable, provided this will not inhibit good rapport. For example, the greeting should not be: 'Good morning. Let me say at once that our charging rates are £X per hour'!

In some cases it will be possible to deal with costs once the solicitor has obtained the client overview (at the 'Preliminaries' stage).

In other cases it will not be possible until after the 'Obtaining the facts' stage and in some, particularly commercial and/or regular clients, it will be perfectly acceptable to leave costs until 'Closing'.

10.6.2 What?

The matters to be covered in the information to be given to the client are laid down in the 'Written Professional Standards (1991)'.

Broadly speaking, the solicitor must inform the client of:

(1) the Green Form scheme;
(2) the Legal Aid scheme;
(3) the firm's hourly charging rates.

For a more detailed study, see the LPC Resource Book *Pervasive Topics* (Jordans 1993) Part II, Professional Conduct.

10.6.3 How?

Costs should be discussed in a business-like way.

The solicitor is providing a service to the client and should not therefore appear to be embarrassed at having to discuss money.

In many cases, particularly litigation, it will be necessary to make it clear to the client that only a rough estimate of the total cost can be given because of the uncertainty concerning the amount of work which may prove necessary and the time it will take.

10.7 FURTHER READING

Students wishing to undertake further reading on the matters covered in this chapter will find any of the following books helpful.

Binder & Price *Legal Interviewing and Counselling* (West Publishing Co, USA, 1977)
Sherr *Client Interviewing for Lawyers* (Sweet & Maxwell, 1986)
Twist *Effective Interviewing* (Blackstone Press, 1992)

Chapter 11

NEGOTIATION

11.1 INTRODUCTION

Solicitors spend much of their time negotiating in one way or another, whether in formal meetings to settle the terms of a company take-over or partnership agreement, or through a series of telephone calls to try to agree a mutually acceptable time and date for the completion of simultaneous conveyancing transactions.

The above two examples of negotiation are both transaction-based. The other common type of negotiation is dispute resolution, where a dispute has already arisen between the parties giving rise to possible legal action (eg for breach of contract, negligence, undue influence on the making of a will, unfair dismissal, ancillary financial relief on divorce, breach of intellectual property rights). In such cases, resolving the dispute by negotiation rather than by litigation can save time and legal costs. It can also reduce animosity. This can be particularly important where the parties will continue to have a relationship after the dispute has been resolved, such as a business relationship or a family one.

Whether it is transaction-based or dispute resolution, the general principles of negotiation remain the same but the specific application of those principles may vary according to the context. Negotiation is an art rather than a science.

11.2 THE ETHICAL ASPECTS OF NEGOTIATING

A solicitor must always act ethically in accordance with the solicitors' rules of professional conduct. A solicitor must never lie, for example by giving false information. However, there is no duty to volunteer information which is adverse to a client's position. If asked a direct question on such a point, the solicitor cannot lie, but he can refuse to answer, or offer no comment, or say 'I have no instructions on that point'. The other negotiator might then, of course, read between the lines of the reply and guess what the true position may be.

11.3 NEGOTIATING STYLES

11.3.1 Categories

Some writers group negotiators into two general styles with names like: hard/soft or aggressive/co-operative.

However, such categorisation can be a misleading division of a myriad of different styles. Figure 1 demonstrates this by charting two characteristics of the negotiator which are not necessarily mutually exclusive but which can be integrated with each other in widely varying degrees.

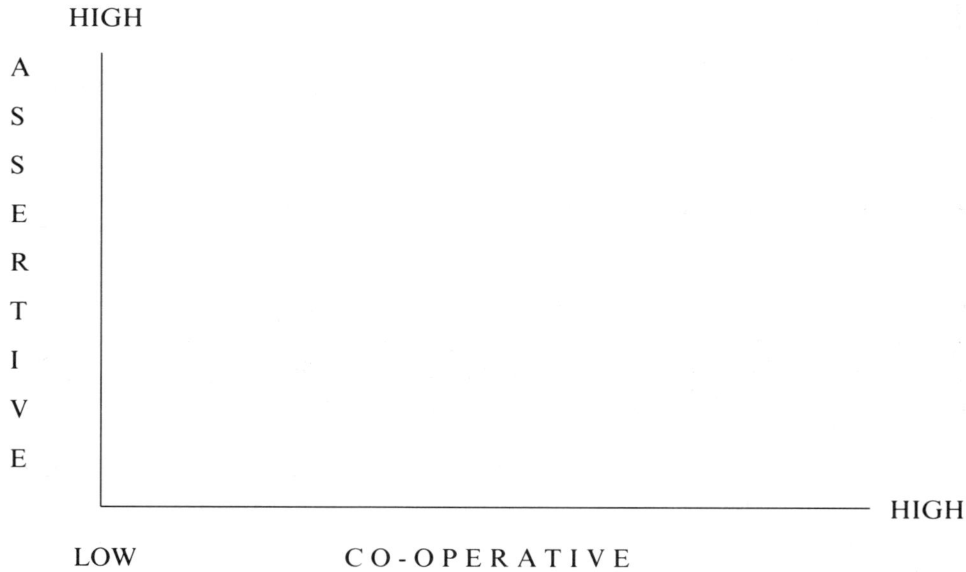

Figure 1

How assertive are you? Mark your point on the vertical axis. How co-operative are you? Mark your point on the horizontal axis. Mark on the graph where your two points meet.

This analysis recognises that everybody's style is different: there are innumerable points on the graph. However, although it gives a general indication of a person's predominant style, the analysis still has inherent drawbacks. First, self-analysis is not always accurate. Secondly, it fails to recognise that you can and should vary your style according to the situation. Effective negotiators are highly flexible and will vary their style according to the merits of the case they are pursuing and the style adopted by the other negotiator.

Figure 2 below shows the same chart divided into five broad styles, any one of which can be used according to the circumstances.

It can be helpful to:

- know the potential strengths and weaknesses of your own predominant style
- assess to what extent you can learn to vary your own style and
- be able to identify, and react appropriately, to the style of the other negotiator

11.3.2 Avoiding

The avoiding style is low both on assertiveness and co-operativeness and is generally to be avoided. It is sometimes used, consciously or unconsciously, by those who are facing actual or potential legal action, or a proposed term in a transaction, against which they have little or no argument. They hope that if they ignore the problem either it will go away or circumstances will change in their favour. If you are acting for the plaintiff or proponent, the appropriate response is to press ahead as quickly as possible.

11.3.3 Accommodating

The accommodating style should generally be avoided – unless, of course, the other side has grossly misjudged the situation and you are only too happy to accommodate them.

11.3.4 Compromising

It is vital that negotiators should have the capacity to compromise; otherwise, deals would never be made and disputes would never be settled. The question is always how and when to compromise. A party may be prepared to compromise in order to avoid:

- the uncertainties of trial (on liability or quantum, or witnesses not coming 'up to proof')
- the delay involved in going to trial
- the emotional stress that continued litigation could involve
- the legal costs of going any further – even if you win in court, you are unlikely to recover all the legal costs from the unsuccessful defendant
- the further loss of management time for a commercial client
- the transaction falling through or
- souring an on-going relationship between two commercial parties or between members of a family

11.3.5 Competing

Competitors are unco-operative and highly assertive. They may or may not also be aggressive.

If you have a strong case and the other side is accommodating, a competing style can be highly effective.

On the other hand, if it is misused, the style can create mistrust, distorted communication, tension and the souring of long-term relationships. It can provoke retaliation (the other side becomes aggressive) or obstinacy (the other side becomes avoiding). In either case, settlement can be severely delayed or a proposed deal can fall apart. Clients will not be grateful.

If you are faced with competitive negotiators, try to avoid such counter-productive though understandable reactions. Ignore the personality and concentrate on the objective merits of the arguments. It may be helpful to ask yourself: 'Why are they behaving like this?' There could be a number of possible reasons, each of which should generate a different response from you.

(1) The behaviour might be part of their personality, their normal style. Have you or any of your colleagues negotiated with them before? Consult as widely as possible.

(2) It may be that they do in fact have a very strong case.

(3) They may have a very weak case and are therefore bluffing or over-compensating. Stay calm. Take care not to react too hastily. Bide your time until you are more certain of the objective merits of the case.

(4) They may be under-prepared. As a result, they may be worried that they are running the risk of making an error of judgment and conceding too much. They therefore over-compensate and become less co-operative and more assertive (or avoiding) in order to reduce that risk. If you suspect this to be the reason, the best tactic might be to adjourn the negotiation until they are better prepared.

(5) They may have become competitive in response to what they perceive to be your competitiveness. There is anecdotal evidence that, after a heated and unproductive negotiation, one negotiator said to a neutral observer: 'I started off

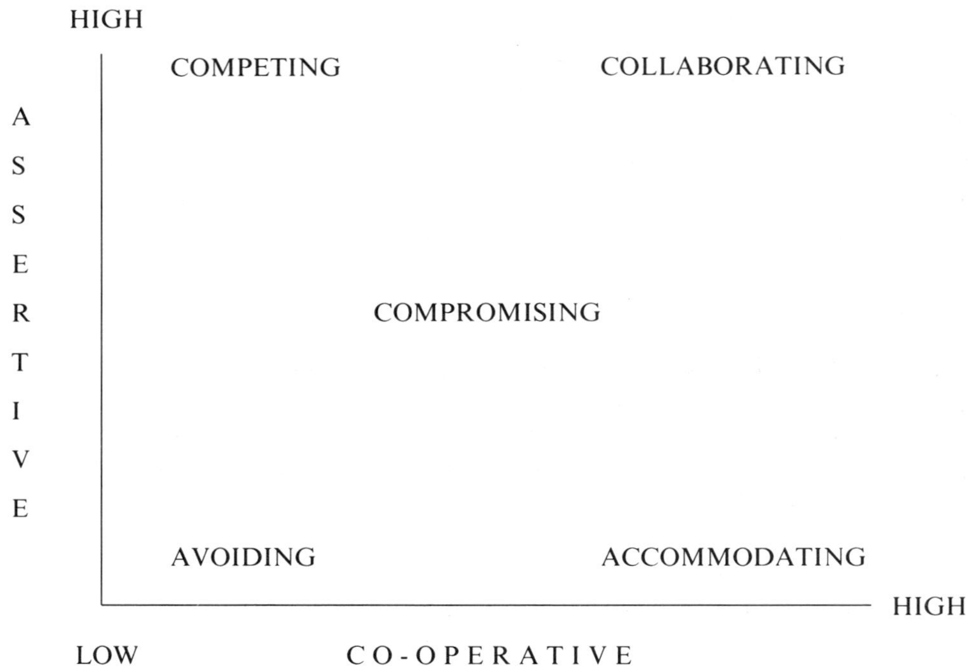

Figure 2

in a spirit of co-operation and compromise; I was prepared to adopt a collaborative search for a mutually acceptable solution; but he was so competitive that we both ended up just going hammer and tongs at each other'. The other negotiator said exactly the same.

11.3.6 Collaborating

Some people call collaboration 'problem-solving' or 'principled negotiation'. In theory, it is often the ideal negotiating style because it gives you the best of both worlds. Assertiveness and co-operativeness are not mutually exclusive. You can be high in both.

Assertiveness is not the same as aggression. You should aim to be sufficiently assertive to press your own client's case and to avoid being trampled on by an aggressive opponent; at the same time, you should be sufficiently co-operative to search for any possibility of a mutually beneficial solution. This is particularly important where there will be (or the parties would like there to be) a continuing business or personal relationship after the present dispute has been resolved.

Beware, however, of certain risks.

(1) Beware of wolves in sheep's clothing, ie the pleasant negotiator who smiles a lot, flatters you, appears to be perfectly reasonable (and may pepper his statements with phrases like 'fair and reasonable' and 'sympathetic to your client's case'), but who on objective analysis is being competitive and offering very little. The moral is: do not jump to conclusions; try not to allow personality to influence you; concentrate on the objective merits of the case.

(2) If you are trying to adjust your own predominant style, for example become more assertive or become more co-operative, there is a danger that, as one characteristic increases, so the other decreases. Although it is possible to be high on both, it can be difficult to achieve.

11.3.7 Conclusion

Everyone has elements of all five styles within them. You should try to be flexible, to exploit your strengths, to minimise your weaknesses, and not to be distracted by personalities. Do not allow your own ego to intrude. Try to think about the case objectively from your client's point of view.

The rest of this chapter generally assumes a collaborative style. However, thorough preparation, self-confidence and perceptiveness are more important than personal style.

11.4 PREPARATION FOR A NEGOTIATION

11.4.1 Importance of preparation

Thorough preparation is vital: 'Knowledge is power'. Research the facts, the law, and the procedure. Have you or anyone else in your firm handled a similar case in the past?

11.4.2 Interests not positions

Look behind the parties' stated positions, ie their stated offers or demands, and try to identify their underlying interests. It may be that the underlying interests can be satisfied in some other way and at less cost than you initially expected. Example situations include the following:

(1) There may be an underlying interest in establishing or maintaining a business relationship.

(2) In negotiating a lease of the major unit in a new shopping mall, the landlord might demand from his major 'anchor' tenant absolute bars on assignment, sub-letting or change of use. The tenant might demand absolute freedom on all three. This presents an apparent impasse. However, the landlord's underlying interest might be to use the anchor tenant to attract 'satellite' tenants to the other, smaller units, while the tenant's interest might be the long-term freedom to move elsewhere. A compromise which might satisfy both parties' underlying interests would be to have a short-term restriction rather than one which lasts for the whole duration of the lease.

(3) In the proposed sale of a business, the seller's solicitor might say, 'My client wants £200,000 for it'. The underlying interest might be either that the seller feels he needs that amount of money to put into another venture or that it is the true value of the business. In the former case, a possible solution would be for the seller to continue to be involved in the business after the sale. This may provide him with further income, while allowing the proposed purchase price to be reduced.

Looking for underlying interests is particularly important in transaction-based negotiations or multi-issue claims. It is less likely to be productive in debt-collection, personal injury or other single issue, 'money only' claims. However, it should always be investigated. For example, in debt-collection it may be that the creditor has an underlying interest in the survival of the debtor's business.

11.4.3 Search for variables

There are often variables which can be brought into play, for example, costs, currency, money-substitutes (goods or services), quantity of goods, quality of goods or services ('specification'), location, time periods, promises of future orders, etc. Thus one party may be able to improve an offer at little cost to himself but the improvement may satisfy a particular interest of the other party.

11.4.4 Packages and priorities

In multi-issue cases, work through the whole package and decide on priorities, for example:

- critical items which cannot be conceded
- items where you would look for success and
- items which are of no great significance to your client

11.4.5 Narrow the issues

Narrowing the issues involves considering likely areas of agreement.

11.4.6 Strengths and weaknesses

Identify your own client's strengths and weaknesses. Which strength are you going to push the most? What information are you prepared to reveal?

Will the other side spot any particular weakness in your client's case? If so, try to predict the questions they might ask, and prepare carefully worded replies. Hesitation or stumbling at the negotiation will not look professional and is likely to betray your weakness.

You must, of course, behave ethically. Any misrepresentation would constitute professional misconduct, as well as rendering voidable any resulting agreement. You have an interest in being trusted.

What are the other side's strengths? Is there anything you can do to counter them? For example, can you obtain other evidence or reinterpret existing evidence?

What are the weaknesses in the other side's claim? Prepare carefully worded questions which will make evasion difficult for them, and press them to reply.

11.4.7 BATNA

One of the best-known books on negotiation is Fisher and Ury's *Getting to Yes*. Their acronym, BATNA, stands for Best Alternative To a Negotiated Agreement, and they recommend that you identify, and develop, your own BATNA and also try to guess the other side's. This should help you to decide your 'resistance point' and protect you from conceding too much. It is not generally necessary to settle at all costs.

A BATNA could be litigation (in which case you litigate and negotiate simultaneously) or capitulation. In transaction cases your BATNA could be to do a deal with a third party rather than with the other side, or not to do a deal at all.

11.4.8 Settlement zones

Can you identify a possible settlement zone? This involves:

(1) deciding on your own client's:
   (a) ideal settlement (first bid);
   (b) liked settlement (what you would be happy to settle for; this could be a number of different packages); and
   (c) current resistance point (avoid calling it 'bottom line' to your client as this might create false expectations: you may have to change it later in the light of further evidence);

(2) making an educated guess at the other side's ideal settlement, liked settlement and resistance point; and
(3) constantly reassessing (1) and (2) in the light of new information.

The settlement zone, if it exists at all, lies between the resistance points of the two sides.

All negotiators go through the above process more or less consciously, but it is helpful to do so methodically.

11.4.9 The forum for the negotiation

The forum for negotiation could be correspondence, telephone, a meeting or any combination of the three.

At the outset, choose the most appropriate medium for your client's case, and then be prepared to change if it proves appropriate. For example, in many cases you might start by using correspondence, but that could later become unnecessarily rigid and time-consuming. It may be wise to suggest a meeting when you have developed a strong enough case to be able to take advantage of face-to-face contact.

Correspondence

Correspondence has the following features:

- it is capable of being orderly and reasoned, and is therefore especially appropriate at the outset of complex cases
- it gives people time to think and therefore to avoid over-hasty decisions
- there is a risk that certain points in a letter may be left unanswered in the reply
- some solicitors find it easier to be assertive
- it contains no non-verbal signals ('body language')
- it can lead to delay – either as a tactic, or because ambiguities or omissions are not rectified immediately and
- it is more difficult to trade concessions

Telephone

Negotiation conducted by telephone has the following features:

- it is quick and useful for resolving one point
- make sure you are properly prepared. It is better to be the person making the call. If you are the receiver, consider saying that you will call back at an agreed time so that you have the opportunity to prepare properly
- there is no body language, but tones of voice are more noticeable. Silences are even more powerful on the telephone than in meetings. Use silence yourself, and do not be tempted to fill silences with a remark you may regret
- some solicitors find it more difficult to be assertive on the telephone than in correspondence; some find it is the other way round
- make an accurate record of what is said

Meetings

Meetings have the following features:

- they are immediate
- they give greater commitment to explore the case thoroughly and/or settle
- body language and silences are readily apparent and capable of use
- they are more fluid and give greater possibilities of fine movements, nuances, and the trading of concessions and

- some solicitors regard the suggestion of a meeting as a sign of weakness; others regard it as a sign of strength

Some solicitors have a fear of meetings because of the possibility of making a decision which is later regretted, or accidentally revealing a weakness, or generally feeling uncomfortable in a potentially adversarial face-to-face role. All of this is quite natural. If, however, a meeting would objectively be in the client's best interests, you should try to overcome any fears by thorough preparation and practice which will increase your self-confidence.

The remainder of this chapter generally assumes that the negotiation will be conducted by way of a meeting.

11.4.10 Preparation for the meeting

Venue

In some fields of law, there is a tradition that meetings will take place at the offices of the seller or plaintiff. What if you have a choice?

Having the meeting at your own firm's premises gives you the feeling of control. You have full access to your papers and to the office's secretarial, catering and other facilities. Also, you do not have to suffer the time, cost and general inconvenience of having to travel.

Attending a meeting at the other side's offices might therefore be a disadvantage. However, the travelling time can sometimes enable you to arrive fresher and more fully prepared. Also, enabling the other side to feel at ease in their own offices might induce them to be more collaborative.

A third possibility is to agree a neutral venue.

Agree the time and length of the meeting

Are you a 'morning' or an 'afternoon' person?

You might want to time the meeting so that lunch will present an opportunity for an adjournment, with the consequent possibilities of review or a more informal continuation of the negotiation.

Attendance at the meeting

How many people from each side will be attending? Find out their names and roles in advance. If a number of people will be attending, who will chair the meeting – the host, the person who suggested the meeting, or some other person?

Will clients also be present? Often, they are present at transaction-based negotiations but not at litigation-based meetings. Sometimes clients sit in separate side-rooms or make themselves available for telephone calls in order to give instructions to their solicitors during the meeting.

It may be a good idea to have clients present at the meeting so that an agreement can be hammered out there and then, particularly if you think:

- the major problem has been a lack of communication between the respective clients
- your own client is being unrealistic or
- the other solicitor is the problem (eg not settling a case which his or her client wants to settle) and

- you can trust your own client (preparation of roles is vital) and
- you trust the other solicitor not to seek to undermine your authority in front of your own client

Conversely, you might not wish to have clients present where there are personality clashes between the different clients or where you have an intimidating client who might hamper your style.

Seating arrangements

Who will sit where? What ambience do you want to try to create? To sit face to face across a table from each other is more likely to appear adversarial, whereas seating placed at a 90 degree angle is likely to appear more collaborative.

Clarify the purpose of the meeting

Is the meeting to be exploratory only, or is there a possibility of settling? If the latter, check that those attending will have authority to settle on behalf of their respective clients.

The agenda

In a multi-issue case, try to agree the agenda with the other side in advance.

If possible, try to arrange the order of issues on the agenda in a way which will enable you to test their negotiating pattern and their willingness to trade concessions before reaching an item which is of critical importance to your own client.

Decide your strategy

Examples of matters you might like to consider are:

- your opening position
- the amount and the sequence of the concessions you might be prepared to offer and
- what disclosure to make and when

However, you should be prepared to be flexible.

Deciding the amount of your opening bid

Should you 'aim high' or go straight to the figure or package which you think is closest to a realistic compromise? The advantage of aiming high is that it gives you room to manoeuvre. It:

(1) guards against the risk of you having been over-pessimistic about the relative strengths and weaknesses of each party's case, their priorities, and the ability of their legal advisers; and

(2) allows you to 'come down' and offer concessions to the other party. This can be an important way of showing the other side that you have listened to and understood the case they have presented at the meeting and that you are prepared to compromise. All compromises require 'give and take'. Compromising allows people to save face. Honour is satisfied. If, however, you refuse to move from your opening figure, the other side may perceive you as obstinate and unreasonable, and therefore refuse to settle, even if you have all the bargaining power or your opening figure is in fact realistic.

Generally, therefore, you should only open at your final figure if:

- that is the tradition or culture in that particular field of law or
- you have a case or bargaining position that is not only strong, but obviously strong

In either case, you should explain clearly to the other side this aspect of your strategy: that it really is a case of take it or leave it.

The disadvantage of aiming high is that if you go too high, you can lose credibility and respect, and drive the other side away from the negotiating table. Aim 'high' therefore means 'highest justifiable bid'.

Which party should make the first bid?

In some fields of law, the person who makes the first bid is determined partly by tradition. For example, in property transactions, the solicitor acting for the landlord or seller draws up the draft lease or contract. In litigation, if the claim is for a liquidated sum (eg a contractual debt), the opening bid belongs to the plaintiff. If the claim is for unliquidated damages, in certain cases (eg personal injury claims) there is an argument that the plaintiff should simply wait until the defendant makes an acceptable offer or payment into court.

Where the position is not clear-cut, the advantages of going first are that it allows you to exert an immediate and powerful influence and it shows confidence. The disadvantage is that you risk misjudging the bid.

Even if you do not wish to make the first bid, you might still like to make the first opening statement, so that you can try to establish the climate of the negotiation.

Final preparation for the meeting

Reread the file, and refresh your mind on key documents, facts, dates and names.

Make sure that you know your client's position on all the possible variables.

11.5 OVERVIEW OF A NEGOTIATION

Every negotiation should have a beginning, a middle and an end. It should be an agreed, structured process (like the order of advocacy in court hearings); otherwise, there is the risk that it will degenerate into chaos, with continual sniping and cross-fire. As a general principle, the wheels of a negotiation are oiled by good structure and management. As with interviewing and advising, structure and management interrelate with personal communication skills: each promotes the other.

Structure	*A possible strategy*
Opening	Aiming high
Discussion and bargaining	Probing Searching for variables Trading concessions Keeping whole package in mind
Closing	

11.6 THE OPENING

11.6.1 Creating the climate

The opening phase of a negotiation is important for two reasons. First, it creates the climate for the negotiation. Patterns, styles and pecking order establish themselves early and are difficult then to change.

Secondly, energy and concentration are high at the outset of the negotiations but later deteriorate.

11.6.2 Ground rules

The host of the meeting should, after effecting any necessary introductions, confirm the ground rules for the meeting, for example:

- the purpose of the meeting
- whether or not it is 'without prejudice' and/or 'subject to contract'
- the likely length of the meeting
- the agenda and
- who will make the first opening statement

11.6.3 Your opening statement

Unless you have sound tactical reasons for doing otherwise, there are some general rules relating to opening statements.

Do:

- consider saying how long your statement will take, if it is likely to be more than two or three minutes
- if your opening statement is going to contain a bid, explain your reasoning *before* disclosing the actual bid. This increases the chances of the other side listening properly to your reasons. Otherwise, they will be thinking about the figure and their response rather than your reasons
- present your case concisely and confidently
- use collaborative tone, posture and gestures (unless you have decided to adopt a competitive style)
- observe carefully the other side's verbal and non-verbal reactions and
- remember the one-third rule (see **9.1**)

Don't:

- express assumptions of the other side's interests and priorities, as this could annoy or antagonise them. Allow them to make their own case in their opening statement
- allow them to interrupt or side-track you
- speak for too long

11.6.4 The other side's opening statement

It is important that you:

- listen carefully – use all the passive listening techniques (see **9.2.1**)
- concentrate on identifying their underlying interests
- evaluate their style
- remain non-committal on their proposals and arguments – indicate understanding, if you can, without indicating agreement and

- take brief notes (this can be a useful way of concealing your immediate reactions)

At the end of their opening statement:

- seek clarification if necessary. Do not allow pride to deter you – you must be sure you understand exactly what they are saying. Negotiations can easily break down because of simple miscommunication
- summarise
- stress areas of agreement
- make sure that they have told you the whole of their 'shopping list', to reduce the risk of being ambushed later by a last minute demand

Do not concentrate too much on mentally drafting or rehearsing your own rebuttal, as this will hinder your listening to and understanding their case, and do not interrupt (unless you have deliberately chosen to be competitive).

11.7 THE MIDDLE PHASE: DISCUSSION AND BARGAINING

> Statements generate resistance
> Questions generate answers
> Silence generates discomfort, answers, new suggestions.
> (adapted from a passage in *Getting to Yes* by Fisher and Ury)

> I don't go in to do all the talking. Quite the opposite.
> I go in to do the listening because that's the best bit.
> (Insurance company chief claims inspector, quoted in *Hard Bargaining* by Hazel Genn)

11.7.1 Discussion

During the discussion:

(1) demonstrate that you have heard and understood what the other side has said even if you do not agree with them;

(2) in the middle phase of a negotiation, you should probe the other side's case with a mixture of appropriate open and closed questions.

You could question any of the following:

- any assumptions you think they might be making
- their underlying interests or needs ('Why does your client want . . . ?')
- whether or not there may be other ways of meeting those interests
- the criteria or evidence to justify their bid ('What criteria did you use to arrive at . . . ?' 'What evidence have you got to support . . . ?' 'Where did you get that evidence from?')
- their interpretation of the law or of the facts or
- analogous or comparable circumstances or cases they have had

Do not ask two questions at once.

Give them time to answer – do not be tempted to fill a silence too quickly.

Listen and observe carefully when they answer. Was there any hesitation, uncertainty or discomfort?

If necessary, re-phrase crucial questions so that all the angles are covered.

Do not allow them to use diversionary tactics such as answering a question with a question, or changing the subject. Be courteous but firm.

(3) spell out the weaknesses of their position calmly and firmly;
(4) be prepared to answer their questions with a judicious mixture of firm replies, silences and counter-questions. Try to maintain a confident tone of voice and posture;
(5) review the progress of the discussions at appropriate intervals. If there is an impasse, or one aspect is taking too long, consider the following:

- defer further discussion of the particular topic until later in the negotiation
- summarise. This can give you the opportunity to stress the areas on which you have already reached agreement and so reinforce the climate for agreement; it can also give you time to think and, if appropriate, to try to redirect the negotiation
- suggest hypothetical or conditional concessions ('If we were able to move on X, would you be able to move on Y?')

11.7.2 Bargaining

(1) Generally, you will only have agreed to a meeting (other than a purely exploratory meeting) if both parties are prepared to compromise, ie to bargain.

(2) Although you might bargain item by item or clause by clause in multi-issue cases, try to keep the whole package in mind. It might be sensible not to finalise an agreement on any particular issue until the shape of the whole agreement is clear (including, for example, costs).

(3) Keep searching for variables, for example: time for payment; payment in a different currency; a promise of future orders or the grant of options; performance-related payments; performance in stages.

(4) Bargaining involves the trading of concessions. Compromise is achieved by both parties moving from their original positions. On the assumption that the other side has aimed high, you should be reluctant to accept their first offer.

A competitive negotiator might refuse to concede anything to you for some time, and then concede only small amounts, slowly and at irregular intervals, and of diminishing amounts. Such a strategy is clearly designed to lower your expectations. However, if in fact there are significant margins between that negotiator's ideal settlement, liked settlement, and resistance point, the strategy carries the risk of a relatively sudden but very late climb-down (eg a 'door-of-the-court' settlement). If you suspect that this strategy is being used against you, consider abbreviating the negotiation and press ahead with your BATNA (Best Alternative To a Negotiated Agreement) – for example, by pressing ahead with the litigation if you are a plaintiff or making a payment into court if you are a defendant.

When you are offered a concession, it is a question of judgment whether you express appreciation for it, or emphasise the lack of cost to them, or both.

When making a concession, emphasise the cost to you of it and try to give a reason for it. For example, you can often relate it to something the other side has said in the negotiation. Your concession can thus demonstrate that you have taken their point and responded accordingly, rather than appearing to be arbitrary.

In order to avoid 'giving away' a concession with nothing in return, or in order to try to move the negotiation forward, always consider offering conditional or hypothetical concessions: 'We could move on X but only if you could move on

Y'; 'I have no authority from my client on this point, but what if X?'. Although these statements might be interpreted to mean that, if pushed, you would be prepared to concede unreservedly, it is a risk that parties have to take in the dynamics of a negotiation.

(5) Make sure you take appropriate notes and, in particular, keep a record of all concessions or agreements.

11.7.3 Adjournments

Adjournments can be very useful.

The length of an adjournment will depend on its purpose. It could be for as little as ten minutes, for example in order to have a brief strategy review (on your own, with a colleague, or with your client), or for as long as several weeks or months in order to await the availability of further evidence.

Other reasons for suggesting an adjournment include:

- alertness waning
- to help resolve an impasse or deadlock
- to allow a heated atmosphere to cool down or
- to try to 'close the deal' during the relative informality of a refreshment break

11.7.4 Resolving deadlocks

In cases of deadlock the following actions should be considered:

- defer an item on the agenda
- search for variables
- adjourn or
- refer to an alternative dispute resolution ('ADR') process (see **11.10**)

11.8 THE END: CLOSING A NEGOTIATION

11.8.1 When?

The timing of the close of a negotiation will depend on a cost-benefit analysis. How much more do you think you can achieve? Compare the expected achievements against the cost to the client in terms of time, money and stress. Will further negotiation be cost effective? This analysis needs to be conducted at regular intervals. Beware of a variation of Parkinson's Law: 'negotiating expands to fill the time allotted to it'.

11.8.2 How?

A number of tactics can be used to signal to the other side that you see the end in sight.

- 'Last rites' – summarise the position reached, emphasising the concessions you have made and the extent and reasonableness of your movement: 'We have reached our final position'
- Use a refreshment break to suggest informally that the end is near
- Give a deadline or ultimatum
- Make a concession and express it as a final gesture to settle
- If the gap between the sides is small, either suggest, or try to induce the other side to suggest, that you 'split the difference'

- If there is one outstanding point, you might be able to agree that the point be adjudicated by an agreed independent third party

11.8.3 The agreement

Do not allow the euphoria of reaching agreement to distract you from other important and immediate tasks, such as:

- confirming what has been agreed
- preparing an immediate agreed written summary
- ensuring that details are clarified in order to avoid later disputes and
- preparing a list of actions to be taken (if appropriate) by both sides

11.9 'DIRTY TRICKS'

The phrase 'dirty tricks' is used loosely, and is not necessarily confined to misconduct. You need to be aware of such tricks, not so that you can use them, but in order to be able to recognise them when they are used against you and, if possible, be able to counter them. They include the following.

Surprise attacks

Surprise attacks can take the form of sudden changes in tactics or demands, intimidation, withdrawal of offers or emotional outbursts. They are often designed to throw you off balance, undermine your confidence, and create anxiety and a desire to placate or settle quickly.

Try to remain unperturbed. Try not to retaliate. If you find it difficult to continue to focus on the merits of the case, consider questioning their tactics openly or calling an adjournment.

'Good guy, bad guy'

The 'good guy, bad guy' tactic is sometimes used by a negotiating team of lawyers, or a solicitor who wishes to portray his client as hard and uncompromising.

The aim of the tactic is to capitalise on the relief felt at evading the 'bad guy'. Again, you should try to continue to focus on the merits of the case.

Feinting

Feinting is where the solicitor seems to attach great importance to one particular item. He then concedes it in order to 'soften you up' for another item in which he expresses little interest but which is, in fact, far more important to his client.

Do not take things at face value.

False deadlines

False deadlines can sometimes be tested by saying 'We might be able to offer more, but we will not know until after [the date of the deadline]'.

Limited authority/reneging on 'agreements'

Always make sure at the time of the agreement that it is explicit whether or not the solicitor has the authority to settle, whether the agreement is final, and record the position in writing. If you do not, you may think that a case has been settled only to receive a letter stating, for example: 'I reported on our provisional agreement. My client is fairly happy with it, but there is just one matter . . .'.

Last-minute demands
Make sure you obtain all the other side's demands at the outset. This will make it less likely that they will surprise you with a sudden new demand.

Environmental controls
If the seating arrangements or environment of the meeting room make you feel uncomfortable, you should immediately and politely ask for them to be changed.

Lying
Try to take accurate notes of key points without being distracted from the negotiation. If you can later prove that the other side lied during the negotiation, then the settlement could be rescinded for misrepresentation and, where a solicitor knowingly lied, the matter could be reported to The Law Society as professional misconduct.

11.10 ALTERNATIVE DISPUTE RESOLUTION

11.10.1 What is it?

Alternative dispute resolution (ADR) is not a term of art: it is simply any process of dispute resolution other than litigation, arbitration or traditional negotiation between the parties or their solicitors.

The object of litigation, arbitration, negotiation or ADR is to provide a process which efficiently and effectively resolves a dispute. Which of the four, or which combination of them, is best will depend on the circumstances of each case.

The essential ingredients of ADR are:

(1) it is a voluntary, private process. The parties cannot be forced to use ADR; if they do use it, they can control the mechanics and rules of the process; and they can withdraw from it at any time unless and until they make a contractually binding out-of-court settlement or agreement;
(2) there is a third party neutral (often a mediator) who facilitates settlement, often by 'shuttlecock' diplomacy, but who has no power to order or impose a solution on the parties.

In essence, ADR is intended to be an efficient and structured form of negotiation involving a third party. It can thus be interposed between traditional negotiating and litigation (or arbitration): if traditional negotiating fails, try an ADR process; if that fails, then either stalemate or litigation (or arbitration) remains.

Although usually used in the litigation field, ADR can also be used in commercial transactions. First, a commercial contract could incorporate an ADR clause, ie a non-binding (but influential) promise that if any dispute later arises between the parties, they will refer that dispute to an ADR process before resorting to litigation or arbitration.

Secondly, if parties are negotiating the terms of a transaction and reach an impasse on one particular term, they could agree to refer that one item to an ADR process.

11.10.2 The advantages

Like traditional negotiating, ADR can be quicker, cheaper and more private, and produce more flexible terms of settlement, than litigation or arbitration.

The third party neutral:

- can provide a view that is perceived by both parties as being more objective
- by shuttlecock diplomacy may be able to identify potential solutions that neither party alone could see and
- has a better chance of preserving relationships between the parties

This last point can be very important in commercial or family disputes, but is less so where neither party has any intention of continuing any future relationship with the other.

11.10.3 The disadvantages

(1) One reason why ADR is relatively quick and cheap is that the evidence is not investigated or examined as thoroughly as in litigation or arbitration: instead, only what are thought to be the key issues and interests are explored. Parties cannot have it both ways, ie a wide, in-depth investigation which is also quick and cheap. In each case, it is a question of choosing the lesser of two evils.

(2) Because ADR is a voluntary process, it is not appropriate when one party needs immediate judicial relief by way of an interlocutory injunction.

(3) Likewise, ADR is unlikely to resolve 'non-genuine' disputes, for example where a defendant is clearly stalling for time and refusing to admit liability simply in order to hang on to his money for as long as possible.

(4) ADR is not appropriate in 'test cases' where you want a binding, judicial precedent, for example the correct legal interpretation of a clause in a standard form contract.

11.11 FURTHER READING

Fisher and Ury *Getting to Yes* (Business Books, 1989)
Scott *The Skills of Negotiating* (Gower Publishing, 1981)
Halpern *Negotiating Skills* (Blackstone Press, 1992)
Genn *Hard Bargaining* (Clarendon Press, 1988)
Kennedy *Everything is Negotiable* (Business Books, 1990)
Williams *Legal Negotiation and Settlement* (West Publishing, WA, 1983)
Foskett *The Law and Practice of Compromise* (Sweet & Maxwell, 1991)
ADR – An Introduction to Alternative Dispute Resolution (The College of Law, 1992)
Lax and Sebenius *The Manager as Negotiator: Bargaining for Co-operation and Competitive Gain* (New York Free Press, 1986)

Chapter 12

ADVOCACY

12.1 INTRODUCTION

In answer to the question 'Are good advocates born or made?', most people would say: 'They're born. Advocacy is not one of those things which can be taught'. Many lawyers would probably say the same. Skilled advocates are seen as being eloquent, articulate, and able to think on their feet: all qualities which at first sight seem to be innate rather than acquired. Undoubtedly, some advocates are more naturally gifted than others, but many of these so-called gifts can be acquired through hard work and practice. Perhaps the worst mistake is to assume that good advocacy is simply a matter of flair, and little else. The advocate who demolishes an opponent's witness in cross-examination rarely achieves this by jumping to his feet and firing off the first thing that comes into his head; a great deal of thought and preparation will have gone into every aspect of the challenge he makes.

This chapter gives a basic introduction to advocacy. For those who wish to practise as advocates, it represents the first stage of a continuous learning process. However, others may never appear before a court as an advocate at any stage of their professional careers. Even so, the skills covered in this chapter will prove useful in any situation where effective oral presentation is required.

12.2 SKILLS

The skills of an advocate divide into oral skills and organisation skills.

12.2.1 Oral skills

Advocates are skilled talkers: this is an obvious point which should never be overlooked. Within the stylised atmosphere of the courtroom the task of the advocate, subject to the rules of professional conduct, is to talk his way to the best result that can be obtained for his client. The three major oral skills are as follows.

Presentation

Every advocate needs to be a good storyteller, especially when he is opening a case on behalf of either the prosecution or the plaintiff. It is not generally realised that a court may know next to nothing about the facts of the case it is about to try or the issues involved: it therefore needs to be put in the picture in a way which will engage its interest.

Argument

Every advocate also needs to be a good persuader. Much of an advocate's time will be spent addressing the court with a view to persuading it to find in favour of his client. Argument may be as to the overall issue of guilt or liability, or as to a subsidiary issue such as bail, the grant of an interlocutory order, or a point of law.

Questioning witnesses

The questioning of witnesses is the skill which young advocates tend to find the most complex and difficult to master. English trials are characterised not only by their adversarial nature but also by the fact that much evidence is still given orally. The ability to extract the relevant evidence from one's own witnesses by means of examination-in-chief and to challenge the testimony of an opponent's witnesses in cross-examination is still seen as the most important attribute of the experienced advocate.

In the course of a civil or criminal trial, all three of the above skills will be exercised, but in many other situations advocacy will consist almost exclusively of presentation and argument. This is particularly true of the vast majority of chambers applications in civil cases, because evidence will almost invariably be given by affidavit. Bail applications and pleas in mitigation in criminal cases also involve very little questioning of witnesses.

12.2.2 Organisation skills

In addition to the oral skills, a good advocate also draws upon other back-up skills which are exercised outside the court room. If one observes an experienced advocate performing in court, it all seems effortless: he has all the facts are at his fingertips, nothing seems to throw him off his stride, and witnesses are examined and cross-examined incisively and in a logical sequence. On top of this, he manages to maintain the appearance of being calm and dignified at the most crucial moments, and never loses his temper. At all times, he is courteous to the court, his opponent, and the most recalcitrant witnesses. To the uninitiated it may look easy, but this level of competence is achieved only by hard work and experience. It is also dependent upon the advocate having thoroughly prepared and organised the case beforehand.

The most important organisation skills are set out below: there is nothing magical about any of them, in fact some of them may appear positively mundane, but no advocate can do without them.

Fact gathering and analysis

No advocate can begin to prepare a case until he has thoroughly mastered its facts. Until this is done, it is impossible to analyse its strengths and weaknesses. Ignorance of the facts will also make it far more difficult to perform adequately in court. For example, when cross-examining a witness it will often be necessary to fire a sequence of rapid questions in order to try and shake his testimony. The task will be made immeasurably easier if the advocate's mastery of the facts is such that there is little or no need to refer to prepared notes before proceeding to the next question. Many readers will have seen US courtroom dramas on television in which advocates never use notes. In real life they are trained to memorise the whole case file. Although UK courtroom style is very different, advocates should try to rely on notes as little as possible.

Knowledge of the relevant law

It is essential to research the relevant substantive law. The advocate must also develop a detailed knowledge of the law of evidence and the relevant procedural law. So far as evidence is concerned, it will always be necessary to study the relevant facts carefully in order to analyse:

(1) what the issues are;
(2) which issues are in dispute;
(3) who has the burden of proof; and

(4) what admissible evidence is available to prove or disprove those issues.

However, that is not enough; you will also need to memorise as much of the law of evidence as you can since an evidential problem may arise unpredictably during the course of a trial. Advocates rarely have time to look the law up in advance of raising an objection.

Similarly, procedural points have a habit of cropping up unexpectedly: an advocate's effectiveness will be greatly enhanced if his level of knowledge is such that these can be identified as soon as they arise.

Handling paperwork

In some respects, handling paperwork is the most neglected organisation skill of all, but it is in fact one of the most important, especially in civil cases. Even quite simple cases can end up producing masses of papers, all of which will need to be referred to at some time during a case. It is important therefore not only to devise a system which enables a required document to be located at a moment's notice, but also to know the contents of every document. This is particularly vital in chambers applications in civil proceedings so far as affidavit evidence is concerned. The Master or district judge may intervene by suddenly asking a question on a particular issue. The advocate should immediately be able to refer him to the relevant paragraph in the appropriate affidavit.

The ability to handle paperwork is also assuming a far greater importance in civil trial advocacy with the introduction of rules requiring pre-trial exchange of witness statements.

12.3 THE BASICS

This section contains a simple checklist to assist in preparation of a case. It also deals with wider aspects of court behaviour and protocol.

12.3.1 Preparation

Good advocacy depends on planning and preparation at every stage. In particular the order in which you address each task needs to be carefully considered so as to achieve the maximum benefit. The following checklist should always be followed.

Master the relevant facts

If the facts are simple, try to commit them to memory. In more complicated cases prepare a written chronology for reference purposes which should ideally then be memorised as far as possible.

Analyse the facts

By applying the appropriate substantive, evidential and procedural law you should be able to identify the following:

(1) the legal issues in dispute. Consider in this context whether there are any submissions you will need to make, for example as to admissibility;
(2) the factual issues in dispute. Identify what findings of fact the court will have to make if your client's case is to succeed;
(3) develop a 'theory' of the case consistent with your client's instructions. The more plausible the case advanced, the more likely it is to succeed.

Based upon the analysis above, plan objectives for each stage at which you will be called upon to speak or examine witnesses.

12.3.2 Presentation

Although presentation has been categorised as a specific oral skill, every aspect of the advocate's courtroom role in effect involves conducting a presentation, not only of the client's case but also of the advocate himself. The following list sets out a number of presentational rules which should always be followed.

(1) Maintain eye contact with the person whom you are addressing.
(2) Never read from a prepared text.
(3) Be aware of 'body language'. The way in which an advocate behaves can affect the court's perceptions of his or her case. Try always to bear the following points in mind:
   (a) Stand still. Advocates who are nervous have a tendency to sway from side to side.
   (b) Stand up straight when in open court. Make sure you know your case well enough to avoid frequent references to your papers.
   (c) Do not speak with your hands in front of your face. This is another common mannerism when a speaker is nervous. Be especially conscious of this trait in chambers proceedings where advocates remain seated.
   (d) Keep your hands and arms still (within reason). Although arm and hand gestures can sometimes be an effective means of emphasising a point they should be used sparingly.
   (e) Keep your emotions under control. To be an effective advocate you will need to be able to hide all kinds of feelings. For example, never appear shocked because a witness says the opposite to what you expect. Learn to sail on unperturbed through the most stormy waters.
(4) Speak slowly in a clear, low tone. If you are anxious, you are likely to speak quickly and in a high voice. In particular, always 'watch the judge's pen'. You are hardly likely to be persuasive if the court cannot keep up with you. The same rule applies when taking the court through documents: it takes time for them to read them and digest their contents.
(5) Do not be afraid of pauses. What may seem to the advocate to be a long gap in presentation is often not even noticed by the court.
(6) Avoid being long-winded and unnecessarily repetitive. These are both traits which suggest that you have not prepared the case very well.
(7) Know your court. All your planning must be with a view to persuading the court of the strength of your case. It is perhaps obvious but nevertheless important to realise that, for example, a judge will need to be addressed differently from a lay magistrate. Tailor your style to suit your audience.
(8) Be honest and courteous. At all times, bear in mind the need to build and maintain your reputation with the court. The advocate who loses the court's trust is of no use to his client. Always be scrupulously courteous to the court and to your opponent, even if you are disappointed with the way your case has gone.

12.3.3 How to address the court

Nothing reveals an advocate's lack of experience more than a failure to adopt the correct mode of address. The following list should therefore be committed to memory:

Court	*Mode of address*
High Court Judge:	'My Lord' or 'My Lady' as appropriate
Circuit Judge:	'Your Honour'
Recorder:	'Sir' or 'Madam' as appropriate
District Judge of the High Court or County Court:	'Sir' or 'Madam' as appropriate
Master of the Supreme Court:	'Master'
Supreme Court Taxing Master:	'Master'
Magistrates (lay and stipendiary):	'Sir' or 'Madam' as appropriate.

In the magistrates' court, 'Your worships' is technically incorrect, but frequently used and indeed preferred by many lay benches.

A particular problem is whether it is appropriate to address the court in the second person singular ('You'). In the case of District Judges, Masters and magistrates, it is perfectly permissible provided 'Sir' or 'Madam' is interposed at appropriate intervals. For example, in a plea in mitigation to a bench of lay magistrates it would be perfectly appropriate to proceed as follows:

> 'Madam, there are three matters relating to the defendant's involvement in these offences that I would like to draw to the attention of you and your colleagues. First, madam, there are two specific aspects of the pre-sentence report which I would like to refer you to...'.

High Court and circuit judges pose more of a problem. As a general rule, 'you' should be substituted by 'Your Lordship(s)', 'Your Ladyship(s)' or 'Your Honour(s)' as the case may be. For example, in the Crown Court before a circuit judge, the previous address would begin:

> 'May it please Your Honour, there are three matters relating to the defendant's involvement in these offences that I would respectfully draw to Your Honour's ('your'?) attention. First, Your Honour, if I might be permitted to draw Your Honour's attention to two specific aspects of the pre-sentence report...'.

To those who are unfamiliar with courtroom protocol, this version may sound unnecessarily obsequious. Nevertheless, this is the level of courtesy expected and you depart from it at your peril. The odd 'you' or 'your' here and there may be acceptable, but do not take risks until you are experienced and know your court.

12.3.4 How to refer to your opponent

It is equally important to extend all the appropriate courtesies to your opposing advocates. Choose from 'My friend' or 'The prosecution/defence' or 'Mr/Ms/Mrs/Miss Smith'. The term 'My learned friend' is traditionally reserved for barristers, although this is no longer a hard and fast rule. If you are opening the case you should always ascertain the name of your opponent since it is a normal courtesy to introduce them to the court. For example: 'Sir, my name is Mr Jones and I appear to prosecute this case and my friend Ms Smith appears on behalf of the defendant'.

12.3.5 Three golden rules when addressing the court

As well as knowing how to behave in court, an advocate must be able to create an impression of being experienced. Failure to observe the following will tend to reveal precisely the opposite.

(1) Do not give evidence yourself

Not only is this improper, it also suggests over-involvement in the client's case. Avoid phrases such as, 'My client tells me . . .' or 'I happen to know that . . .'. However, it will often be necessary to put the client's views to the court, for example in a civil chambers application or a plea in mitigation in a criminal case. In chambers applications the phrases, 'I am instructed that', and 'my instructions are', are perfectly acceptable, but in criminal cases they are sometimes interpreted as being coded messages that the advocate does not believe a word the client is saying. Phrases such as, 'I have discussed this with my client and he wants you to know' or, 'My client wishes me to inform you,' are more appropriate.

(2) Do not give your opinion

Avoid using phrases such as, 'In my opinion . . .' or 'I think . . .'. When an advocate wishes to persuade the court to adopt his view of the case, phrases like, 'I submit,' or, 'I would seek to persuade you,' or, 'I would urge you,' are more appropriate. The important thing to remember is: the only opinion that counts is that of the court.

(3) Object rarely, but quickly

There is an enormous temptation, especially when you have thoroughly researched a case, to object at every opportunity. Indeed this often impresses the client. However, it will not endear an advocate to the court unless the point is one of substance. Do not object unless the point advances your case or diminishes that of your opponent. Be alert: the decision to raise an objection will often be a split-second one, especially if it involves the issue whether an inadmissible question has been put to a witness.

12.3.6 Five golden rules when questioning witnesses

Although the examination of a witness is as much an art as a science, the following are basic rules for questioning witnesses which apply whatever the nature of the proceedings.

(1) Keep your questions short

Formulate questions so that, ideally, they do not exceed ten words. If the question is convoluted there is a risk that neither the witness nor the court will be able to follow it. Nothing takes the wind out of an advocate's sails more than being asked to repeat or re-phrase a question because it is incomprehensible.

(2) Ask one question at a time

For reasons similar to those given above it is essential to refrain from asking multiple questions. The last thing you want is for your opponent to rise to his feet and say, 'Madam, I wonder if my friend would be kind enough to indicate to the witness which question he wants him to answer first'.

This means that a quite simple point may often need to be broken down into several questions before it can effectively be put to a witness. For example, if you are seeking to extract a concession from an identification witness that she was standing 50 feet away, it was dark and it was raining, etc, you may need to ask a whole series of short questions in order to succeed in this objective.

(3) Know your objectives in respect of each witness

This applies as much to your own witnesses as to those of your opponent, but is particularly important when planning a cross-examination.

(4) Try to avoid asking questions in cross-examination to which you do not know the answer

This rule should not be taken too literally because sometimes one has no choice but to probe. The main thing is to ensure that you are never floored by the unexpected. For example, let us assume that you are cross-examining an identification witness on the issue of where she was standing at the time of the incident. If you were simply to ask 'Where were you standing?', you would have no control over the answer. Contrast:

Q. You said earlier that were standing on the corner of Main Street and Underwood Road didn't you?
A. Yes.
Q. And there's no dispute, is there, that that is about 50 feet from the incident you say you saw?

Even if the witness says 'No', you have much more control over where to proceed from there. Alternatively, if you can easily prove that the witness was standing 50 feet away, you could quite safely ask the question 'Where were you standing?' because you know that if the witness were to reply 'About 6 feet away', you would have plenty of ammunition with which to contradict her.

(5) Know when to stop

There is always a danger in going on for too long, but it is particularly important not to fall into the trap of asking one question too many. It is a great temptation to press on when you have a witness 'on the run'. However, that is the time to pause and reflect briefly upon whether, having secured some favourable concession, it might not be wiser to refrain from cross-examining further.

For example, if you have managed to extract from the identification witness referred to above concessions that she was standing 50 feet away, it was dark and it was raining, it is a great temptation to then say with a final flourish: 'So how can you be so sure it was the accused that you saw?'

This is the one question you (and your client) may live to regret!

12.3.7 Witnesses: court formalities

There are a number of matters of court protocol concerning witnesses of which you need to be aware, especially since it will be your task to explain them to your client and other witnesses before they give evidence.

Criminal cases

In a criminal case, witnesses other than the defendant should be asked to stay out of court until called.

If the defendant is to give evidence, he must be called before other defence witnesses.

Witnesses may refresh their memories from their written statements prior to being called to give evidence. Other parties must be informed if this has taken place.

Civil cases

In a civil case, witnesses may sit in court throughout the hearing. If the advocate wishes to exclude witnesses from court, he must apply for an order to that effect.

The plaintiff and defendant are both usually called first by their advocate.

Witnesses may refresh their memories from their written statements prior to being called to give evidence. Other parties must be informed if this has taken place.

12.4 OPENING THE CASE

This section considers opening speeches in all types of proceedings. Although the length and purpose of such speeches may vary widely, they are all vitally important. They provide the advocate with an opportunity to make the first impression. This can be vital, as the court or tribunal may know little or nothing about the case they are about to try. For example, in a chambers application the Master or district judge may only have had time to skim through the affidavits beforehand; in a criminal trial before magistrates, the bench will probably know nothing about the case other than details of the charges.

12.4.1 The order of speeches

Criminal trials

The prosecution always has the right to make an opening speech before calling its evidence. In simple summary trials, this right is sometimes waived. If the prosecutor does open, he will usually:

(1) introduce himself and his opponent to the court;
(2) take the bench briefly through the charges; and
(3) outline the facts of the case and the evidence that he intends to adduce in order to prove the charges.

The opening speech requires the advocate to be a good storyteller so that the relevant incidents are brought to life. If there is an item of evidence for which admissibility is in dispute, the prosecutor has two options: he can make no mention of it when opening, leaving admissibility to be determined at a later stage; alternatively, admissibility may be determined as a preliminary issue before the case is even opened.

Defence advocates rarely make an opening speech before calling their evidence, because by doing so they lose the right to make a closing speech. Since the prosecutor has no right to a closing speech, the defence advocate will usually take advantage of having the last word.

Apart from the right to make speeches, either advocate may at any stage make a submission on a point of law. In particular, the defence may submit that there is no case to answer at the close of the prosecution case. In such an event the opposing advocate always has a right to reply.

Civil trials

The plaintiff's advocate has the right to open (unless, unusually, the burden of proof of all issues lies on the defendant). As judges now have power to dispense with opening speeches, their use may decline, but the practice of handing in a written 'skeleton argument' to the judge in lieu of an opening speech is likely to increase. As in criminal cases, if the defendant's advocate elects to make an opening speech, he is not entitled to make a closing speech except with leave of the court.

The purposes of the advocate's opening speech in a civil trial will be to:

(1) introduce himself and his opponent to the court;
(2) indicate the nature of his claim, for example: 'Your Honour, this is a claim for damages for breach of contract';
(3) summarise the areas of dispute between the parties;
(4) outline by reference to the pleadings the alleged facts of the case (nothing which cannot be proved should be asserted), indicating areas of dispute;
(5) introduce the evidence, including any matters contained in agreed documents;
(6) summarise the legal principles involved, indicating areas where a ruling will have to be made.

12.4.2 Chambers applications in civil cases

The procedure in chambers applications is an important topic for trainee solicitors, because this is where they will gain their first experience of advocacy. It should be noted that the procedure differs from that in trials. The advocate's purposes will be to:

(1) introduce himself and his opponent to the court;
(2) indicate the orders he is seeking by reference to the application or summons;
(3) outline the nature of the claim by reference to the pleadings (if any);
(4) ask the court whether it has read the affidavits and, if not, ask the Master or district judge whether he wishes to be taken through them.

The procedure is more fully considered at **12.11**.

12.5 EXAMINATION-IN-CHIEF

Examination-in-chief is in many respects more difficult than cross-examination because an advocate should always be seeking to succeed on the strengths of his own case rather than the weaknesses of his opponent's. Accordingly, the way your own witnesses give their evidence has a vital bearing on the overall impression that your case creates in the mind of the court.

12.5.1 The characteristics of examination-in-chief

Although, with one exception, advocates have a complete discretion as to the order in which witnesses are called, it is usual in civil cases for the plaintiff or defendant, as appropriate, to be called first. In criminal cases, the prosecutor will usually call the victim first, but the defence advocate is obliged to call the defendant before other witnesses as to fact unless the court directs otherwise (Police and Criminal Evidence Act 1984, s 79). The advocate calling the witness will, as a matter of courtesy, begin by announcing each witness in turn, for example, 'Your Honour, I now call the plaintiff, Margaret Brown'.

The principal objectives of examination-in-chief are to:

(1) present the witness's evidence in a logical sequence (usually chronological or by topic);
(2) cover all the relevant issues upon which the witness is able to testify; and
(3) anticipate matters likely to be raised in cross-examination.

The major characteristic of examination-in-chief (and what makes it so difficult for the advocate) is that the witness must, so far as possible, be left to tell his own story with minimal prompting from the advocate. In order to achieve this objective, leading questions are not generally permitted, neither will the witness normally be allowed to refer to any previous written statement made by him (unless it qualifies as a contemporaneous note).

Although there is a degree of controversy over what constitutes a leading question, the generally accepted definition is that it is a question which suggests its own answer by seeking to put words into the witness's mouth. For example, if an advocate was seeking to establish that a witness saw the defendant, James Smith, in 'The Mitre' public house at midday on Monday 24 August 1992 (all of which is in dispute) it would not be permissible to ask: 'Did you see James Smith in 'The Mitre' public house at midday on Monday 24 August 1992?'.

Instead, the advocate would need to proceed by means of a number of non-leading questions as follows:

Q. Can you remember what you were doing on Monday 24 August 1992? (This question is arguably leading, but probably not objectionable.)
A. Well, let me see. Oh yes, I went into work in the usual way.
Q. Did you stay there all day? (Non-leading)
A. No, I went out for an early lunch.
Q. About what time was that? (Non-leading)
A. Oh, about ten to twelve I think.
Q. And where did you go? (Non-leading)
A. A pub called 'The Mitre'.
Q. Did you see anyone there you recognised? (Non-leading)
A. Yes, I saw James Smith . . .

and so on. As can be readily appreciated this technique requires the advocate to prepare very carefully in advance to ensure that he is able to guide the witness through his evidence without resorting to prompting.

The technique also requires stamina, since it may take time even to elicit a simple set of facts in this way. The only three occasions on which leading questions are permitted by way of exception are:

(1) when the witness's evidence relates to a matter that is not in dispute;
(2) where a denial is invited from the witness; and
(3) on those rare occasions when a witness is declared to be hostile.

An example of exception (1) above would arise if the only dispute was as to the date on which the witness saw James Smith:

Q. Do you recall an occasion when you saw James Smith in 'The Mitre' public house? (Leading, but not disputed)
A. Yes.
Q. And can you remember when that was? (Non-leading)
A. Yes, it was on Monday 24 August 1992.

The advocate should always check in advance with his opponent as to what matters can be led to the witness. Matters such as name, address and occupation may always be led, but some advocates prefer to ask witnesses to state these details in their own words to help put them at their ease.

An example of exception (2) would be if Mr Smith's advocate was seeking to extract a denial from his client. It would then be permissible to proceed as follows:

Q. Mr Smith, were you in 'The Mitre' on Monday 24 August 1992 at midday? (leading)
A. No, I was not.

Exception (3), namely the hostile witness, is rarely encountered. It is considered in outline only.

12.5.2 The witness who does not come up to proof

Criminal cases

If the witness displays an unwillingness to tell the truth at the instance of the party calling him, the court may declare the witness to be hostile. This allows the advocate who has called him to ask leading questions and, with leave, any previous inconsistent statement made by the witness may be put to him. Such a statement may only be used to discredit the witness's testimony: it is not independently admissible. Further discussion of this difficult technique is not appropriate at this stage.

In most cases, however, the witness failure to say what the advocate is hoping for is the result of forgetfulness, incompetent examination-in-chief or a poorly taken statement. In such a situation witnesses cannot be cross-examined. The advocate can only try to repair the damage by calling additional evidence which supports his case. The problem of the forgetful witness may also be avoided if a contemporaneous note of his earlier evidence is available (see **12.5.3**).

Civil cases

The position of the hostile witness in civil cases is broadly similar to that in criminal cases, with one major exception: the court can be invited to treat any previous inconsistent statement as admissible evidence in its own right and, if appropriate, prefer it to the witness's oral evidence (Civil Evidence Act 1968, s 3).

If the witness is not declared hostile, the advocate's options are limited in the same way as in criminal cases (but see **12.5.3**).

12.5.3 Introducing documents and real evidence

Documentary evidence may be introduced for a variety of reasons. The term 'document' includes items such as photographs, tape recordings, video films and computer data. From an evidential point of view it is important to remember not only that a document's authenticity must be established, but also that its contents must be admissible for the purpose for which they are tendered. The rules differ materially in criminal and civil proceedings.

Criminal cases

A witness must normally be called to prove the authenticity of any document which is to be adduced in evidence. Although documents cannot be agreed (contrast the position in civil cases), in practice many documents, such as agreed plans of traffic accidents, are routinely admitted. Copies of the documents are generally sufficient (see Criminal Justice Act 1988, s 27). A police officer will normally be called to prove the authenticity of a defendant's written confession. This will be done by asking the officer to identify the defendant's signature and recount the circumstances in which the statement was made. If accepted, the original will be admitted as an exhibit. The police officer will then normally be invited to read the defendant's written confession to the court. Although most interviews with suspects are now tape-recorded, the written summary of the interview will basically be proved in the same way.

The other commonly encountered document is the 'contemporaneous note'. The basic rule is that a witness may, with leave of the court, refresh his memory in the witness box from any document which was made or verified by him substantially contemporaneously with the events to which he testifies.

Police officers, in particular, will frequently ask for leave to refresh their memories from notes contained in their pocket books, but other witnesses may also be permitted to refer to their original statements.

The advocate conducting the examination-in-chief will question the witness in order to establish whether the document falls within the rules. The opposing advocate may then cross-examine the witness solely on that issue. Only after leave has been granted will any further evidence-in-chief be given by the witness. The opposing advocate is entitled to inspect the document and may cross-examine the witness about its contents, subject to certain technical rules which are outside the scope of this chapter. Although witnesses are not otherwise allowed to refer to their written statements in the witness box, the court does have a discretion to allow a witness to leave the witness box to read his statement (*R v Da Silva* [1990] 1 All ER 29). When the witness resumes giving evidence, it must be given orally without further reference to the statement.

Real evidence consisting of other objects, for example a weapon, must likewise be proved by a witness who can show that they are what they purport to be and that they are relevant to the issues. It will also be necessary to prove that an appropriate chain exists which links the object to the accused.

Civil cases

In theory, a witness must be called on to prove the authenticity and originality of each document which is to be adduced in evidence. However, in civil cases, documents are almost invariably agreed. They will usually be put in as one or more agreed bundles by the plaintiff's advocate in the course of his opening speech. Furthermore, the use of documents is inextricably bound up with the rules as to discovery, expert evidence and exchange of witness statements, all of which are outside the scope of this chapter.

The rules as to the use of contemporaneous notes to refresh the memory are the same as in criminal cases. In addition, the same general rule applies as in criminal cases: witnesses may not refer to their written statements when giving evidence. However, there are two exceptions. First, as in criminal cases, the court has a discretion to allow the witness to leave the witness box to consult his proof. Secondly, the court can use its discretion under the Civil Evidence Act 1968, s 8 to admit the witness' written statement even though the normal notice requirements of s 2 have not been complied with.

12.6 CROSS-EXAMINATION

Effective cross-examination is generally regarded as representing the highest level of advocacy. The skilled advocate, by harrying his opponent's witnesses with probing questions, can effectively demolish the other side's case. However, it is an art hedged with misconceptions, most of which derive from watching too many fictional courtroom dramas. The aggressive language and sarcastic manner that are characteristic of the television soap opera are usually inappropriate in the real world.

Cross-examination is a vast topic which deserves a book to itself (many such books have been written over the years). It is also a skill which requires constant practice. The basic principles can be stated fairly briefly, but detailed examination is outside the scope of this chapter.

12.6.1 Defining objectives

Advocates should always give careful thought to what they hope to achieve by cross-examination. In order to do this effectively, it will be necessary to develop a 'theory' of the client's case. This theory should be a plausible version of the events, consistent with the available evidence and the client's instructions which, if accepted, will result in the court finding in the client's favour. Once the advocate has developed this theory, he will find it easier to work out his tactics.

Another point to be borne in mind is that, whatever tactics are to be adopted, the cross-examining advocate must always 'put his case' to his opponent's witnesses. In other words, the advocate must confront his opponent's witnesses with all aspects of the client's case which conflict with their evidence. This need not be done directly. One often hears advocates saying, 'I put it to you that...' as if it were an essential ritualistic device. However, it is possible to be more subtle than this. For example, using the illustration in **12.5**, if Mr Smith's advocate needed to put to the witness that it was in fact on 25 August 1992 that he saw his client in 'The Mitre', it would be permissible, but inadvisable, simply to state: 'I put it to you that you are mistaken, it was on 25 not 24 August that you saw Mr Smith in 'The Mitre', wasn't it?'.

If the answer were to be 'No', that would be the end of the matter.

Suppose, however, that the cross-examining advocate knew that the witness regularly went to 'The Mitre' at that time: the client's case could be expressed more effectively in the following way:

Q. It's true, isn't it, that you regularly go to 'The Mitre' for lunch?
A. Yes.
Q. At about the same time each day?
A. Yes.
Q. Around midday?
A. Yes.

The cross-examiner could continue by trying to establish that there was nothing special about 24 August 1992, before suggesting to the witness that he had in fact got the day wrong and that he had seen the accused on a different day.

In other respects the cross-examiner has considerable freedom of manoeuvre in deciding how to structure his cross-examination. There are four main questions to consider.

(1) Should I cross-examine at all?

It may well be that unless the advocate needs to put the client's case, it is better to ask no questions at all. This is especially so if a witness has not directly damaged the case. Cross-examination may increase the risk of eliciting unfavourable material that would otherwise not come out.

(2) Are there any favourable matters that I can extract?

It is far better for an advocate to get a witness on his side, than to confront him. For example, in a case involving disputed identification, try gently to elicit concessions from the witness that it was, for example, dark and raining at the time, rather than suggest aggressively that his evidence is worthless.

(3) Is there any way in which I can discredit the witness' evidence?

Witnesses can, and often do, make mistakes or erroneous assumptions that can be exposed by cross-examination. Very few witnesses deliberately give false evidence. This always needs to be borne in mind when probing for weaknesses. Again, an indirect rather than a confrontational approach is likely to yield better results. Exposing inconsistencies by reference to a previous inconsistent statement is a particularly effective method. It is governed by special legal rules which are outside the scope of this chapter.

(4) Is there any way in which I can discredit the witness himself?

It is rare for the advocate to find himself in a position to insinuate, for example, that the witness is biased. It is a particularly risky tactic when done on behalf of a defendant in a criminal trial because of the dangers of falling foul of the Criminal Evidence Act 1988, s 1(f)(ii). In any case, the tactic should never be adopted unless there is independent evidence available to substantiate the allegations.

The above four questions are not mutually exclusive: a cross-examining advocate may wish to adopt those parts of a witness' testimony which favour his client whilst challenging other parts which do not. This is a highly skilled and complex operation.

12.6.2 The technique of cross-examination

The major difference between examination-in-chief and cross-examination is that the advocate cross-examining is permitted to ask leading questions. This is a particularly valuable right since it enables him to retain tighter control of the witness than is the case with non-leading questions. However, leading questions should not be used to excess since this may give the impression that the witness is being brow-beaten. The tactic can, however, be particularly effective when an advocate wishes to expose inconsistencies or illogicalities. The trap can be set by asking the witness a series of non-leading questions on peripheral matters as a preliminary to confronting him with weaknesses or inconsistencies in his testimony by means of a series of tightly controlled leading questions. This is a highly skilled exercise.

Two general examples will suffice. Suppose that you were trying to discredit the testimony of an identification witness. There would no doubt be a number of matters which you had thoroughly researched beforehand, such as where he was standing, how far away he was from the incident, the time of day, the weather conditions etc. You would no doubt wish to keep tight control of this part of your cross-examination by means of leading questions. However, it might also be appropriate to probe into what the witness had been doing beforehand by means of non-leading questions. For example, you might ask: 'Now Mr Smith, you say you were on your way home when you witnessed this incident; where were you coming from?'.

The answer might be: 'I'd been down 'The Mitre' for a drink'.

Not all cross-examinations will yield such promising results, but it can be seen that much useful information can be gleaned from peripheral matters by means of non-leading questions without running any risk to one's case.

A second example might be in the case of a witness whom an advocate wished to confront with a previous inconsistent statement. It might be appropriate to begin by inducing him by means of non-leading questions to embellish his story still further before confronting him with his inconsistencies. This is a particularly effective technique where the allegation is that the witness is biased.

12.7 RE-EXAMINATION

Once cross-examination is completed, the advocate who called the witness has the right to re-examine. That right is limited in that: first, he may only deal with matters raised in cross-examination; and secondly, leading questions are not permitted. Very few advocates are skilled re-examiners. It is a sophisticated art. As a general rule, it is most unwise to re-examine unless you are absolutely certain as to your objectives. Its principal function is to repair any damage done in cross-examination, by giving the witness an opportunity to explain or qualify his previous answers. It is useful where, for example:

(1) cross-examination has confused the witness;
(2) the cross-examiner has attempted to impeach the witness' credit;
(3) the cross-examiner has elicited only partial details of an incident which appears to favour the opponent's case.

12.8 CLOSING THE CASE

Closing a case can be more difficult than opening, because a greater degree of improvisation is required. An opening speech can be worked out in detail beforehand: by the time an advocate rises to make a closing address, all the evidence will be before the court and the case may look very different by then. However, it is rare that the central issues will have changed, only the details. It is absolutely vital, therefore, to have identified the likely issues and evolved a 'theory' of the case in advance. It is only in this way that a closing address can deal with all the outstanding issues in a coherent and persuasive manner. It is important to remember that, just as the advocate who opens the case has the advantage of the first word, so the closing speaker is the last advocate the court will hear before retiring to consider its verdict.

12.8.1 Who closes the case?

Criminal cases

The basic rule in summary trials is that only the defence will make a closing speech. The only exception is in those rare cases where the defence has both opted to make an opening speech before calling its evidence and been given leave to make a closing speech. In such a case, the prosecution is also permitted to make a closing speech, but the defence will still address the court last.

Civil cases
Except where the defendant began or where the defendant calls no evidence, the advocate for the plaintiff has the last word in a civil case. If the judge says that he does not wish to hear a closing speech, then the plaintiff has probably already won.

12.8.2 The purpose of the closing speech

Criminal cases
Be brief. Magistrates' courts are very busy places and you will be well advised to confine yourself to the essential points which advance your client's case. However, the experienced advocate will not allow himself to be rushed. If you need a few moments to compose yourself and go over your notes, do not hesitate to ask for them. You should always cover:

(1) any relevant points of law;
(2) the key issues in dispute;
(3) any part of the evidence which weakens the prosecution case and strengthens that of the defence.

Avoid saying too much about the burden and standard of proof. Magistrates need little reminding of this. It is better to concentrate on those parts of the evidence which genuinely raise a reasonable doubt.

Civil cases
The position in civil cases is broadly similar to that in criminal cases, except that an advocate must always be aware that he is addressing a judge, not magistrates. Modify your style accordingly. Since civil trials still take place on the pleadings, a closing speech which follows the issues raised by the pleadings will greatly assist the court. Judges are particularly grateful to advocates who not only summarise the issues that are still outstanding but also emphasise the essential findings of fact which the judge will have to make in order to decide the case.

12.9 ETHICAL ISSUES

An advocate's reputation with the court is his or her most valuable asset. An advocate who has lost the court's trust through some piece of unethical conduct is a liability. Accordingly, the following rules of conduct should be observed at all times.

12.9.1 Criminal cases

Duties of the prosecution advocate
The duties of the prosecution advocate are:

(1) to ensure that all relevant facts and law are before the court;
(2) to make available to the defence any evidence obtained which may assist them, including any previous statement which is inconsistent with the evidence which a prosecution witness gives at the trial.

Duties of the defence advocate
The duties of the defence advocate are:

(1) to say on a client's behalf all that the client would properly say for himself;
(2) to keep confidential all information received about a client and his affairs which the client wishes to keep confidential;

(3) to ensure that the prosecution discharges the onus placed upon it to prove the guilt of the accused. The defence advocate is entitled to put the prosecution to proof even if the defendant has admitted his guilt;
(4) to disclose to the prosecution and to the court all relevant cases and statutory provisions relating to the case, even if unfavourable to the defence. However, unfavourable evidence need not be disclosed;
(5) not to participate in a positive deception of the court. A solicitor may not continue to act for a client who misleads the court (eg by giving a false name, or giving evidence which the advocate knows to be untrue) unless the client is prepared to reveal the truth;
(6) not to act for two or more clients whose interests are in conflict, even if invited to do so by the court.

12.9.2 Civil cases

Advocates for the plaintiff and the defendant are bound by the same rules which are:

(1) to ensure that all relevant facts and law are before the court;
(2) to say on a client's behalf all that the client would say properly for himself;
(3) to keep confidential all information received about a client and his affairs which the client wishes to keep confidential;
(4) where relevant, to ensure that the opponent discharges the onus placed upon him by the burden of proof;
(5) to disclose to the court all relevant cases and statutory provisions relevant to the case, even if not favourable to the client. The advocate may then seek to show that decisions which are against him are erroneous, not binding, per incuriam, or distinguishable. As in criminal cases, the theory is that unfavourable evidence need not be disclosed. However, the rules as to discovery and exchange of witness statements are such that, in practice, both parties may be required to disclose such evidence;
(6) not to participate in a positive deception of the court. A solicitor may not continue to act for a client who misleads the court (eg by giving evidence which the advocate knows to be untrue) unless the client is now prepared to reveal the truth;
(7) not to act for two or more clients whose interests are in conflict.

12.10 CRIMINAL CASES: BAIL AND MITIGATION

A detailed study of criminal advocacy in bail applications and pleas in mitigation is outside the scope of this chapter. However, a very basic guide to the skills required is set out below. Because most criminal advocates will begin their careers with a simple bail application or plea, it is often erroneously assumed that this is 'easy' advocacy. Nothing could be further from the truth: there is nothing easy about a situation in which the client may face a period in custody if his advocate fails him.

12.10.1 Bail

The skills of the advocate will only be required when the application is opposed. Although bail is always ultimately a matter for the court, it will normally be granted as a matter of course unless the prosecution objects. Since defendants have a right to bail prior to conviction and sentence, it is customary for the Crown Prosecutor to begin by formally setting out his objections by reference to the prescribed criteria in the Bail Act 1976, Sch 1, Pt II. The objections will almost invariably be based on an assertion that there are substantial grounds for believing that the accused will either abscond and/or commit further offences while he is on bail. The risk of the accused interfering with witnesses is also frequently advanced as an objection.

The task of the defence advocate is twofold. First, he should seek to put forward arguments which tend to minimise the risks adverted by the Crown Prosecutor. Thus, for example, if the prosecution claims that there is a substantial risk of the accused absconding, this might be rebutted by arguing that:

(1) the accused is pleading not guilty and the evidence against him is weak;
(2) the accused's record (if he has one) reveals that he has never absconded whilst on bail in the past;
(3) even if he is convicted, the likelihood of a custodial sentence is remote.

These are very general illustrations: each case must be dealt with on its own facts. Whatever the facts, thorough preparation is always essential.

Secondly, the advocate must neutralise any substantial risks by putting forward a sensible package of conditions, such as a surety combined with a condition of residence, which will be sufficient to persuade the bench that they can afford to take a risk and grant bail. Although the Bail Act 1976, s 4 is supposed to secure a right to bail, in reality if a prosecutor raises substantial grounds for withholding bail the defence advocate has a difficult task upholding that right. An effective application, therefore, requires as much advance preparation as the circumstances permit. The Crown Prosecution Service (CPS) should always be approached (in advance if practicable) in order to obtain as much information as possible about both the offence and the accused.

If possible, you should obtain detailed instructions from the client concerning his personal circumstances and the existence of any potential sureties. It may be that this will avoid a contested application altogether. If you can produce an appropriate package of conditions to the CPS before the hearing, you may be able to persuade them to withdraw their objections. So far as the actual application itself is concerned, an advocate should always bear three things in mind.

(1) Structure the application in such a way that each prosecution objection is countered in a logical sequence, and conclude with any package of conditions you wish to put forward.
(2) Keep the application as short as circumstances permit and remember that courts usually have a long list of cases to hear.
(3) Tailor the application to the individual client. Magistrates are often offered the same platitudes whatever the nature of the application such as: 'My client strenuously denies the charge, has a fixed address and instructs me that he has been offered work on a building site'.

The statement may be true, but it is vitally important to interest the court in your client's personal circumstances. It might therefore be more appropriate to explain a little more about why your client's denial is so significant. For example:

> 'Sir, if I might begin by referring you to the case against Mr Smith, you will see that it is tenuous in the extreme. The evidence consists solely of hotly disputed identification evidence' . . . and so on.

12.10.2 Pleas in mitigation

As with bail applications, advance preparation is essential. Courts can only sentence on the basis of information and, although the sentencing court may have a written pre-sentence report (PSR) available (this is mandatory when the court is considering a custodial sentence or certain types of community penalty), there will often be a great deal of further relevant background information which the defence advocate can put before the court. The emphasis of the defence advocate's speech has been changed as a result of the Criminal Justice Act 1991, which places the seriousness of the offence at the forefront of the matters to which the court must have regard when passing sentence. Nevertheless, the court is not precluded from considering the circumstances of the individual offender by way of mitigation. The following eight points should always be considered when preparing a plea.

(1) Thoroughly research the realistic sentencing options available, referring, where appropriate, to relevant statutory or judicial guidelines.
(2) Take as full a statement as possible from the client, dealing with the circumstances both of the offence and of the client.
(3) Obtain an up-to-date copy of the client's criminal record, and deal thoroughly with the circumstances of any offences which the court may regard as being 'aggravating' within the Criminal Justice Act 1991, s 29(2).
(4) If a PSR has been ordered, try to contact the Probation Service in advance of the case to see if they will discuss its contents informally.
(5) Arrive at court in plenty of time so that you can discuss your mitigation speech with the client and obtain his approval of your proposed course.
(6) When called upon to address the court, invite them to read any PSR first.
(7) When the court has read the PSR, begin your speech by dealing with matters which affect the seriousness of the offence. Then go on to deal with matters of general mitigation, referring where appropriate to the PSR. Never read paragraphs of the PSR aloud, because the document is confidential. Instead, invite the court to consider the appropriate paragraph. For example: 'Madam, you will recall that Mr Smith's family history is dealt with at the top of page 2 of the pre-sentence report. I would particularly draw your attention to the matters dealt with in paragraph 3 . . .', and so on.
(8) Conclude by 'showing the court the way home'. In other words, if you can suggest a realistic sentencing option which the court can take, you are not only discharging your duty to the client, but also assisting the court. Sentencing an offender is never easy, and anything which helps the court discharge this onerous duty will be gratefully received.

12.11 CIVIL CASES: CHAMBERS APPLICATIONS

12.11.1 Key characteristics

It is particularly important to master the skills relevant to chambers applications in civil cases, because trainee solicitors have full rights of audience before Masters and district judges in chambers. All chambers applications, whether in the High Court or the county court, share a number of common features.

(1) There are no 'live' witnesses. All the evidence will be in affidavit form. Hence the principal tasks of the advocate are to present his case and to argue for the order sought.
(2) Advocates are generally seated.
(3) The proceedings are heard in private.

12.11.2 Preparing for the application

Although the subject-matter of an application may vary considerably from case to case, there are a number of steps which should always be taken.

(1) Try to agree as much as possible in advance. In the case of applications for directions this may produce the result that attendance can be dispensed with altogether.
(2) Make sure all relevant affidavits are filed before the hearing. Although the court may be prepared to accept a late affidavit, it will not endear you to it. In addition, it may result in your client being penalised in costs.
(3) Make sure that you have mastered the facts of the case and that you are familiar with the contents of the pleadings and the affidavits. It is not uncommon for the Master or district judge to deal only with those particular points in the case which he considers need arguing. Your grasp of the facts and documentation therefore needs to be such that you can locate them instantly.
(4) In the High Court, make sure that you have the original writ and relevant pleadings to hand in to the court along with the original summons. There is no court file as such (unlike in the county court). You will also need to ensure, therefore, that you have a complete set of copies to refer to during the hearing. In the county court, copies of the summons and pleadings will already be on file.
(5) Prepare brief notes. Although you should never read out your submissions, it will help you to have a list which summarises the main facts and sets out the points that you intend to raise and to write out a very brief summary of the contents of each paragraph of the affidavits. This need be no more than a sentence or two, but it can be of great help when the court suddenly fires a question at you. An example of such a note in a contract case might be: 'Plaintiff's Affidavit: Para 3 – Summarises the dispute as to time of delivery'.

12.11.3 Conducting the application

Whether the plaintiff or the defendant is the applicant, the party whose summons or application it is will begin. The order will be the same whether the proceedings are in the High Court or the county court and is as follows.

(1) The applicant formally introduces himself and his opponent and then opens the case in the manner described in **12.4**. In applications for summary judgment the plaintiff must do this even if the defendant has not attended. If the case is in the High Court, make sure you hand in the original writ, the pleadings and the summons before you begin. Where your opponent does not attend, you must be able to prove service.
(2) If the Master or district judge asks you to take him through the affidavits, you should do this at a sufficiently slow pace to enable him to digest their contents. It is not normally necessary to read them out verbatim, you should merely summarise each paragraph. Ask your opponent if he wishes to take the court through his affidavit evidence himself or whether he is happy for you to do this.
(3) Once the court has read or had read to it the affidavit evidence of both parties, the applicant will argue for the order sought on the basis of the issues identified in the affidavits. You should anticipate and deal with all disputed matters revealed by your opponent's evidence.
(4) The opposing advocate now addresses the court in similar terms to the applicant. It should be borne in mind that, in applications for summary judgment under the Rules of the Supreme Court, Order 14 or the County Court

Rules, Order 9, rule 14, the burden of proof is effectively on the defendant to establish that there is a 'triable issue'.

(5) The court then considers the evidence and orders accordingly.
(6) The parties make representations as to costs.

Although the subject-matter and nature of chambers applications cover an enormous range, it is vitally important for the advocate to make his submissions as clearly and concisely as possible in order to help the court, especially since it will have to hear so many applications during a working day.

There are many applications in which affidavit evidence will not be required. Those most commonly encountered are time summonses and directions appointments. The same level of preparation is nevertheless required.

12.12 CONCLUSION

Although this chapter could not deal in detail with the subject, it has provided an introduction to some of the salient features of the advocate's art. It should also have made clear the fact that many of the skills of the advocate can be acquired through study and observation. Remember that thorough preparation is the key: without that, no advocate can be fully effective – however fluent his or her oral skills may be.

INDEX